How to
Write
Like a
Writer

ALSO BY THOMAS C. FOSTER

How to Write Like a Writer

A Sharp and Subversive Guide to
Ignoring Inhibitions, Inviting Inspiration,
and Finding Your True Voice

Thomas C. Foster

HARPER ● PERENNIAL

NEW YORK ● LONDON ● TORONTO ● SYDNEY ● NEW DELHI ● AUCKLAND

HARPER ● PERENNIAL

HarperCollins books may be purchased for educational, business, or sales promotional use. For information, please email the Special Markets Department at SPsales@harpercollins.com.

FIRST EDITION

Designed by Jamie Lynn Kerner

Library of Congress Cataloging-in-Publication Data has been applied for.

ISBN 978-0-06-313941-1 (pbk.)
ISBN 978-0-06-313945-9 (Library edition)

22 23 24 25 26   LSC   10 9 8 7 6 5 4 3 2 1

For Frederic J. Svoboda, Hemingway scholar,
teacher extraordinaire, fellow carpooler,
and one of the world's great wheel men

Contents

How to
Write
Like a
Writer

Introduction

Can't We Just Text or Something?

[Writing] cannot be taught, but it can be insinuated.
—THEODORE ROETHKE

CLANG! THAT'S THE SOUND of a basketball hitting a rim. Hard. And clang again. And again. Way back in the mistiest of times, when I was a graduate student, several of us got together on Sunday mornings with a few faculty members, all of us from the English department, for pickup basketball games. To say that it was a group of disparate talents is an understatement. Some of us had played in high school. One or two had been college athletes in some other sports. Some had limited athletic experience. One of my friends, it turned out, had never played the game, and he taught me something I had forgotten: basketball is hard. For one thing, one team is trying to dribble, pass, and shoot while another is attempting to keep the first from dribbling, passing, and shooting. In addition, though, each of those offensive skills is technically challenging, shooting in particular.

Which is where Marty, the friend in question, comes in. His

shooting technique consisted of launching the ball with considerable energy directly at the front rim. This approach, for those of you who don't know, is perfect for producing the loudest possible clang. And it did. So one Sunday I took him aside for a little quality time with the ball. I explained that in order for the ball to fall through the hoop, it had to at some point be above it and permitted a downward flight. He caught the idea of shooting in an arc instead of a line pretty quickly, and with a bit of practice, he began to make some shots. Now, he was never going to be Larry Bird, but neither were the rest of us, and that's fine. Shooting is only one of many necessary skills in basketball, but we can agree it's a fairly important one.

Over the years I found myself thinking of Marty when student writers engaged in self-sabotage, slamming their verbal shots against the front rim. Watching their struggles made me consider how they got that way. Suppose that, rather than just celebrating the ability to drop a ball through a rim, Marty had needed to study the calculus involved in describing parabolas, had needed to work out the numbers on a ten-foot shot as against a seventeen-foot shot. Or that he had been submitted to a barrage of rules on all the things he wasn't allowed to do or was required to do before his shot would count. What are the chances he would ever see that first ball swish through the net?

That's the situation most beginning writers have found themselves in down the decades: you can't write yet; first you have to learn the rules. And what a lot of rules there are—no split infinitives, no ending sentences with prepositions, no fragments, no use of "I" or "me," your introduction must be shaped like this or that, there must be this many paragraphs in the body of your essay, your conclusion must have X number of sentences in it, your research paper must be this tall.

How much anxiety have we burdened would-be writers with before anything gets written, even before such niceties as *ideas* are introduced into the conversation? And what effect does this freight have on those who need to write?

Paralysis. Insecurity. Inadequacy on an industrial scale.

Someone or something—the culture, the educational system, parents, teachers—has so saddled young writers that they cannot communicate effectively with others in their native language. We have tied them in knots. Somewhere between their brains and the page or screen, something dreadful happens. Their fingers get all tongue-tied, and words stammer and stagger out disconnectedly. Or they rush headlong into stream-of-consciousness word salads where angels fear to tread. Or they throw linguistic spaghetti against the wall in hopes that something will stick, the results existing without, in the words of Agatha Christie's Hercule Poirot, order or method. This situation is intolerable.

How did we get into this sorry state?

There are as many answering voices as there are observers and analysts. Listen and you will find a lineup of the usual suspects: the death of regular and sustained reading, too much screen time, bad instruction, social media (that root of all evils), a divorce between most people and the written word, the decline of newspapers and newswriting, maybe even poor potty training. I believe, however, that the main culprit is duress. Between the ages of five and, say, twenty-two, the only experience the vast majority of people have with writing is by coercion. Mostly, that force is imposed by schools, but sometimes it comes from familial pressure (Dear Aunt Mary, Thank you for the handkerchiefs I needed them very much. I am fine how are you? Love, Mikey). The result of all this compulsion is that most people never write for their own purposes, never find pleasure or joy or creativity through writing, never experience *fun* via playing with words. Is it any wonder their efforts sound like cries for help?

Nor does that requirement to write vanish because one turns eighteen. The world beyond high school is filled with required writing: lab reports, research papers, annotated bibliographies, analyses of Episode Five of *Ulysses*, job applications, engineering reports, soccer club bylaws, mission statements, performance reviews, obituaries, public relations releases, eulogies. The world, it seems, is crammed with writing that is no fun and not optional, that must be done no matter how the hapless writer feels about it.

Is it any wonder that any writing task fills so many people with dread? It's about time we brought them in from the cold and let them find fulfillment in writing from inside themselves. Better still, it's time to produce a generation of developing writers with the confidence and ability to generate their own writing and believe in it.

We can't snap our fingers and eliminate the five-paragraph theme or the what-I-did-on-my-summer-vacation essay or the report on soil samples, not to mention the obligatory note of thanks to aging relatives, but we may be able to invest them and other writing necessities with meaning beyond the assignment affliction.

More to the point, however, we teachers and learners and lifelong practitioners of written communication can begin to make onerous tasks a little less so by making the work meaningful for the individuals undertaking them, by locating the "I" at the center of "writing." Just what does that injection of the personal entail? For one thing, it means that we create space for the intelligence and personality and the language of the writer to flower within the task. This re-centering often goes by the name "voice," but the writer's voice divorced from all else can become precious self-indulgence. Beyond that, understanding that there is an "I" responsible for writing a document, it becomes self-evident that there must be a "thou" out there somewhere who exists and who—possibly also under compulsion—will read those words the writer produces. Even essays on standardized tests or state assessments must have readers; a long-ago colleague had been one while in graduate school. When we look at it from this perspective, we see what we should know already: every writing act is at bottom an exchange between two persons, one writer and one reader. Even audiences of millions are simply audiences of one, repeated again and again.

Writing has too often been approached as a set of skills to be perfected or even formulas to be copied and applied as needed. The results, more often than not, are stale, pallid, and halting. Think of whatever version of the five-paragraph theme you were taught at school. At their best, those efforts produce perfunctory but rarely inspired compositions; at their worst, lifeless attempts to copy a pattern. In all its variations, the goal of the five-paragraph theme was never to encourage literary brilliance but rather to impose order on the adolescent brain. Yet many of us go through life thinking that such imposition is the only way to write and that we have somehow failed to grasp it instead of understanding that it was the instruction that failed us. Young people and adults alike deserve better.

I'm not going to lie to you: writing has its good days and bad days. The bad days feel like swimming in molasses, or maybe just drowning in it. There is no way, you think, that the good days can make up for this misery. But then a good day comes, or maybe just a good couple of hours, and that erases all the harshness and self-loathing, and you think, maybe I'm not so bad at this. You feel fulfilled and successful and even, once in a while, brilliant. Because you are. Even then, you know that the dark times are as near as tomorrow. It will go that way as long as you write. The failures may come more often than the successes, but they won't stop you, because the feeling of winning is addictive, because expressing yourself is rewarding in its own right.

The point is, the act of writing should not in itself be drudgery. If it is, you're not doing it right, and I can guarantee that's not your fault. That's what this book is about. Writing is, and will always be, hard work. As with any human activity, it requires discipline, commitment, ingenuity, and thought. Talent doesn't hurt, but those other things can overcome shortcomings in that department. At its best, like basketball, writing should be fulfilling and enriching. You will get better with practice, and practice will be easier if you get a sense of the rewards. I want you to learn to write like a writer, which is to say, to *write like you mean it*. Once you manage that, the rest is just details.

Swish.

WHY WRITE?

1

The "I" at the Center of "Write"

You have to follow your own voice. You have to be yourself when you write. In effect, you have to announce, "This is me, this is what I stand for, this is what you get when you read me. I'm doing the best I can—buy me or not—but this is who I am as a writer."
—DAVID MORRELL

THE MOST STRIKING FEATURE of writing anxiety is the way it manifests as a lack of confidence, a sense that the writer is somehow unworthy of the task. The great writer and writing teacher Gail Godwin personifies that feeling as "The Watcher at the Gate," a voice telling you that you're a nobody, that you have no right to this story or this argument or this fact, that you need to delay until you discover that detail or the full name of that writer. Her Watcher, she tells us in the essay of that title, is an enormous time-suck, constantly pulling her away from her chosen activity (writing) to take care of peripheral tasks, often of no importance. My Watcher wants another pot of tea when I'm already waterlogged. But Watchers can be more pernicious, stealing your self-assurance and stopping your word-flow with doubt. I think that, at its base, the Watcher wants to make you feel too unimportant to write anything worthwhile.

Don't let it.

You are the most important being in your writing world.

There is no writing without a writer, a person with consciousness and conscience, intelligence and knowledge, experience and imagination, uncertainty and confidence. If that writer is you, you are due congratulations: you are the only writer in the history of the earth who has been or will be precisely you. No one else will ever write exactly what you will, because no one will possess those skills, that intelligence, that experience, or that imagination. Your writing can be as distinctive as you are. This is what becoming a writer entails, discovery of the unique qualities in one's work. That awareness drives much of one's writing so the discovery process is of paramount importance.

One of the most damaging myths that writing instructors have historically imprinted on students is that writing is somehow impersonal. And in a very few types of writing, that is mostly true. Newswriting is best done from an objective and impersonal stance: just the facts, get in and out, hit the five Ws (who, what, where, when, and why), avoid personal entanglements. University regulations (something with which I have been intimately acquainted) are so impersonal they even lack agency. The writing is without personality and written in the passive voice: "If the student commits X offense, he or she shall be removed from the university." Really? And just who will be doing the removing? Colleges don't say because that puts them in the position of looking like the bad guys; that is why they never say, "We're gonna get you, sucka."

In most human communication, however, the writer is more present in the writing. Sometimes painfully present. We know within a page, sometimes less, whether that page is by Dickens, Hemingway, Twain, or J. K. Rowling. I could spot writing by D. H. Lawrence, one of the most distinctive stylists ever, a hundred yards away. In the dark. With my eyes closed. Okay, you say, but those are fiction writers. What about nonfiction, which is what most of us write? Even if we leave out the New Journalists— Hunter S. Thompson, Tom Wolfe, Joan Didion, and all those others who developed this new genre in the sixties—whose work is all personality and style, we will see that the vast majority of nonfiction writers do not erase themselves from their work. This is clearest in essays, sermons, and opinion pieces, where the stated goal is to express the ideas of the writer, but writers of nonfiction are present in their style, their ideas, their narrative approach, in virtually every aspect of their work. They may not make showy displays in the manner of Thompson or Didion, but their presence is unmistakable.

Nor is the presence of the writer a modern phenomenon. If we go back to the great preacher-orators of, say, the Colonial American church, they were totally invested, whether in sermon, letter, or essay. Indeed, sermons were often printed and distributed so that they formed the basis for civic discourse; in other words, these men of God meant for their words to live on past Sunday dinner. If you were to read Jonathan Edwards's "Sinners in the Hands of an Angry God," and I hope you will sometime for stylistic and structural reasons and not because you are a Puritan, you will come away in no doubt either that Edwards is front and center in his composition or as to what he thinks. Much the same is true of early secular writers: they oozed personality. Our first great autobiographer, Benjamin Franklin, constructs a fully clothed (and invented) version of himself to narrate the story of his life. He is not Benjamin Franklin but "Benjamin Franklin," and the quotation marks make all the difference. The nineteenth century in Britain was a great age of the essay, and while the language may sound somewhat quaint to our ears, contemporary readers will not have any trouble distinguishing among, say, Thomas Carlyle, John Henry Newman, Thomas Babington Macaulay, and John Ruskin. Their attitudes, their diction, their styles fit them perfectly, even if they feel somewhat heavy and stiff to us.

In fact, nearly the only place in the writing universe, aside from those examples I gave earlier, where "I" is historically unwelcome is in the writing classroom. There are reasons that this should be so, some rational and some less so. Yes, some students will rely on the first person excessively if allowed to do it at all, but that has always struck me as a pedagogical problem and not an existential issue to be avoided. No one wants essay after essay littered with "I think," "I believe," and the lamentable "it's only my opinion," along with dozens of their rhetorical cousins. The difference between the constructions "Franklin adopts his narrative strategy" and "I think Franklin adopts his narrative strategy" is one of argumentative power. In appending "I think" to the declarative statement, the writer has weakened the force of the assertion. Is that weakness fatal? Probably not, but neither does it accomplish any useful purpose. It limits the power of the statement, something almost no teacher of writing has ever wanted for his or her students. Which leads to one of the Foster Rules: **whenever possible, make the subject of your thought the subject of your sentence**. Lots of other instructors have that one, too, only maybe not in bold fonts. In doing that, writers can avoid the first person without having some inflexible rule. Making "Franklin" rather than "I" the subject of the sentence creates a more direct, dynamic statement. That's a good thing, by the way.

So what's the problem with not using "I"? Nothing at all. This is a problem not of usage but of perception. In prohibiting the first person, teachers and guidebooks can unwittingly squeeze the person out of the writing. Instructors hear: don't do anything to make your essay weak, spineless, and flabby. Students hear: don't be present in your writing. The result can be work that is so impersonal and neutral that it could have been written by a machine—and not a particularly smart one.

We want an essay, a newsletter, a movie review that is a conversation, admittedly a little one-sided, between two human beings, two intelligent, thoughtful, engaged persons in the act of sharing information. That cannot happen if one side of that equation is a machine; only a person can sound like—and, more importantly, be—a person. Readers are canny folks: they know if the writer is present or not, and if not, they are likely to check out themselves. "Why should I bother," they ask, "if you don't?" And that is a question you never want your reader to ask. You want to draw them in with your first sentence, hold them throughout your performance, and only release them after your last sentence. Any wobble in the writer's performance risks losing the audience. John Gardner calls fiction "a vivid and continuous dream" and asserts that anything, whether inconsistent character behavior or weak prose or narrative confusion, that breaks the dream is a fatal flaw. We are chiefly discussing nonfiction here, but the same principle applies: don't lose your readers.

What are the implications for keeping the "I" at the center of "write"? Readers are looking for a voice that talks to them from a place of control and confidence. That voice may express anxiety or a lack of conviction, but it should seem in control of what it is expressing. So here is the question: When are you most confident and in control? I submit that it is when you are most yourself. Here are some ways to go about that:

- **Know thyself.** This was the first of three maxims inscribed in the portico of the Temple of Apollo at Delphi, the place where the oracle issued her pronouncements. Not knowing oneself can have disastrous consequences. Just ask Oedipus, whose lack of self-knowledge managed to destroy his entire family. Embedded in that maxim was the concept of knowing one's limits, of not trying to seem more than you are. That works for writers, too.

- **You are not a machine.** A lot of people seem to think that "writing" as they understand it (meaning something better done by people other than themselves) is best when it's impersonal, formulaic, rigid. No, the best writing comes from one person and is offered to another. Be one of those people.

- **Don't hide your light.** Let the real you shine through. This doesn't mean starting every sentence with the first person singular or bragging yourself up. But it is okay to have a writing personality, to not erase yourself from your writing. If this is a conversation between two people, it is rather important that the first person show up.

- **All writing is an act of imagination.** Use yours. Discover or invent the best way to say what it is you have to say in your writing. Don't write the way you think a book would have you do it. Write the way you think and feel will best do the job. Readers can never be happy if the writer isn't. And they can tell.

These precepts are broad for a reason. The bottom line here is that your attendance is requested; it can't be *your* writing without *you*.

There are many aspects of you as a writer. One of them is your *idiolect* or *personal lexicon*. An idiolect is like a dialect in that it encompasses vocabulary, grammar, and (in speech) pronunciation, except that it applies not to a whole region or group of language users but to only one user of a language. In linguistics, "lexicon" refers to the entire store of words in a language. You have just learned two things about me as a writer: first, that I am the sort of English user who can produce "idiolect" without blushing, and second, that I am quite comfortable stealing a word like "lexicon," yoking it to some other word such as "personal," and rendering a different meaning from its standard intent. That's me, a regular linguistic vandal.

What we're talking about here is your whole presentation of language, not only which words are in your storehouse but also what order you put them in and which rules of grammar (official ones or your replacements) you operate under. That's why we can't just speak of "vocabulary," along with the fact that the word conjures up images of Monday word lists and Friday quizzes over "mundane" and "diurnal." So why does your idiolect (and no, it does not involve "idiot") matter? It is a large part of who you are as a writer. More to the point, it is the part that you want to be aware of as a writer: What is my "home" language? How do I sound when writing comfortably? Or formally? As with everything to do with language, your idiolect is dynamic; that is, it will change with your age, education, reading habits, new activities or hobbies, even acquaintances. I have, in the course of my professional life, used the words "heuristic" and "propaedeutic." This is not a confession that makes me proud, but these are part of the lexicon of the higher reaches of literary study, so they can't be avoided in some parts of the field. The nineteen-year-old version of me who was declaring his English major was still a few years away from hearing either of them. You can, of course, deliberately expand your personal lexicon, but a lot of the growth there comes from life experience, which is really the most secure way to remember new words. By all means, though, find out what you sound like at *your* best, not at my best or Hemingway's best or your really smart best friend's best. You can nudge your best to higher levels little by little. That's the best way. Huge leaps lead to huge stumbles. Be your best here, today, in this moment.

Oh, what do those two jawbreakers, "heuristic" and "propaedeutic," mean? Trust me, you don't want to know.

And another thing about the sound of you, just a teeny-tiny recommendation: **burn your thesaurus**. Burn that devil even if it's online. Look, I have nothing against expanding your word hoard; when it comes to words, I think the more, the merrier. It's just that there are two kinds of thesaurus users, those who scarcely need it and those who need something else first. To profit from one, the writer has to not only know the words in question but understand just how they might or might not apply in a given situation. If you lack that understanding, that's a problem.

In fact, I put the word "problem" into multiple thesaurus sites. Here's a partial list: complication, trouble, dilemma, dispute, headache, issue, obstacle, question, box, mix-up, muddle, mess, snag. Seriously, "headache"? There may be a context in which the two are synonyms, but if you try "headache" in a hundred spots where you have used "problem," you'll find that you need several hundred more before you hit the one where the substitution can be made. Meanwhile, in any of the others, you would look purely foolish. Here's how unlikely that situation is to arise: if you swap the words in the same site that came from and enter "headache," you will not find "problem" as a synonym. Now, that's a problem. Or perhaps a headache.

Too often, tentative writers wanting to sound impressive will go fishing for big words to replace small ones. The result? They sound anything but impressive. You don't need that. You only need to sound like yourself, maybe slightly improved. By all means, go looking for synonyms, but stick to ones about whose true meaning you are certain. Variety is good, right up to the moment when it turns weird. If you have the discipline to reject synonym suggestions that don't seem right or that you don't know for sure how to use, the thesaurus can be your friend. Until then, burn, baby, burn.

Same thing with prose style. If you incline toward short sentences—and most people do—don't decide that readers will like you more if you produce long, involved ones instead. Those very complicated structures can get away from inexperienced writers, sometimes even experienced ones, so they require practice in writing them before you unleash them on an unsuspecting public. If you want to master the art of long, involved sentences, you will need to practice them in situations where the stakes are low. In private. But don't be afraid of your natural strengths, whether they are short sentences or long ones.

We will return to sentence structure later on, but for now, let's note that your sound needs to be your sound—with some variation. The standard-issue subject-verb-object, seven-to-nine-word sentence is the main course of the English communication feast. We can't live without it. On the other hand, we do need periodic relief from it. Too many short, declarative sentences stacked up one after another begins to feel very choppy. Readers need to be rescued from that pattern every once in a while. More importantly, writers need for readers not to feel bored or jarred by the rhythm of the prose. Introductory phrases like "More importantly" help with that bumpy-road feeling that short sentences can impart. So do compound sentences, where the writer takes two short sentences and joins them with a comma and a conjunction, like "and" or "but" or "or." From there, writers can vary sentence rhythms by changing whole sentences into *subordinate* or *dependent* clauses that can't stand on their own as sentences (usually by removing either the subject noun or the main verb) as well as by embedding phrases inside the sentences. The sky really is the limit when it comes to ways of varying sentence patterns, but it is well to remember that even in the sky one can fly too near the sun and end up crashing into the sea.

I see what you mean about very short sentences. What happens if you write too many long ones?

Readers fall asleep. Or they lose track of the meaning and give up. Fixing that problem is easy: write shorter sentences once in a while. The smoothest flowing prose is usually a mix of short, long, and medium sentences, with transitions easing the breaks between them.

The most crucial element of a personal style is that it reflects your tendencies as a speaker of the language in terms of vocabulary, sentence structure, rhythm, and sound, while remembering that too much of even a good thing is still too much. Make your writing reflect your personality, but not slavishly so. You need to sound like you, present your thoughts, use your perspective, and generally reveal yourself as a writer. You are never going to be someone other than you, so why would you want to pretend to be? Whoever you are, that will be plenty good enough.

2

I–Thou Relationships

I can't write without readers. It's like a kiss—you can't do it alone.
—JOHN CHEEVER

ALL THIS TALK OF centering yourself in your writing begins to sound too self-involved. Me, me, me, that's all that matters! Out of my way! Well, no. For writing to be published, by which we mean it leaves the hands of the writer to become public, there has to be a second person. Otherwise, it remains private forever, like a diary or journal entry. Which is fine if the thing you are writing *is* a diary or journal. For most of us, however, we write expecting an audience.

We write, for the most part, to make ourselves heard. Every written transaction requires two parties, a writer and an audience. Even if the audience is a single person. The writer must discover how she will relate to various audiences. Articles for professional journals will sound different from those for a general readership, and still more different from love letters to a very special person.

How do we learn to relate to the various groups and individuals who may be our readers at different times and in different venues? How do we learn to marshal the elements of writing—voice, tone, use of evidence, and so on—to accommodate different readerships? For that matter, how do we think of those relationships? We very much want readers, so shouldn't we show some consideration for them?

The first thing to note about audiences is that they are all different, and not only because they are made up of different persons from one venue to another and one time to another. Beyond that, however, it is probably wrong to speak of any written work having *an* audience. If we stop and think about it for a moment, it becomes clear that what you think of as your audience is actually an average of each individual reader in that group. You don't have a single audience of thirty readers but thirty separate audiences of one who, taken together, can be thought of as one entity. Each of those thirty persons will have his or her own reaction to what you've written. There will be commonalities among them, but part of what guides their responses will be their own life experiences, their own points of view on the topic at hand—in other words, whatever they are bringing to the party. You can't control that part, by the way, nor should you worry about it; all you need to do is take care of the parts you do control. If your audience was composed of thirty different individuals, the response(s) might be different, however subtly, and there is no way to plan for that.

Nor can you account for how writing will be received in different regions or countries. As I said a bit ago, audiences vary from place to place and time to time. It is unlikely that an article praising the Yankees will be as well received in Boston as it will be in New York. My advice is to write about the Tigers; only fans in

Detroit will be annoyed by that. The larger issue here is that you can only know your audience down to differences that become too granular for writers to consider. Within small groups, you can relate to nearly everyone who will read your work. Students in your course, for instance, will have individual histories but also a shared history of *this* course, *this* school, *this* community. You can work with that. Always remember, your main duty is to them, however they are constituted. **For the time that you are writing, your reader is the most important person in your life.**

I first discovered what it meant to have an audience when I wrote for a weekly newspaper. Prior to that, my "audience" was always the person standing in front of the class, about whom I knew as little as, and maybe even less than, my students would one day know about me. Remember, instructors at one time were not big on sharing their own lives with their students. It was a more reserved time. Just imagine, a historical moment when no one had ever taken a selfie! To be sure, our teachers and professors had provided plenty of feedback on our writing, but it tended to be, in my case, how little I seemed to understand First Corinthians or the niceties of comma usage. It turns out to be quite hard to warm up to such an audience, even if they provide, as one freshman seminar instructor did, a full typed page of praise and correction for each student's weekly essay.

Among subscribers of the *Argus-Sentinel*, however, there was an immediate sense of reader response. I was the beat reporter for my old high school football and basketball teams. The gig was straightforward: attend the game on Friday, talk to the head coach by phone on Sunday night, and show up Monday morning at the newspaper office with a sheaf of papers detailing story-and-statistics versions of the latest encounter. I remember my first contact with a reader, the mother of a friend. She said she liked the article and added something I hadn't expected, "You sound just like yourself." That hit like a thunderbolt, which in its plural form was the team's nickname. *I* sounded like something? I apparently did, since I heard that comment from a number of readers, not all of whom were relatives. Wow! I sounded like me. And there were people who noticed!

That this was a revelation will tell you something about my writing history to that point. My writing in high school and college was as other-directed as it could be. My goal was to gain approval from someone who, from my perspective, was setting the rules for this game that I was compelled to play. The entire process seemed mysterious—what did they want, what would impress them, how could I avoid annoying them—and entirely external to me. I later realized, when I became the person on the opposite side of the lectern, that I had been unfair to both parties: to me by not understanding how much control I did have and how important my choices were on everything from subject to structure to diction, and to my teachers and professors by not giving them the respect due to a reader. When I talked about writing with my classes over the years, I developed a bit of patter about how they didn't respect me—fear, yes, as the guy who would determine their grade, but not respect. For them as writers, we professors were simply part of the furniture. We were contractually obliged to read whatever they submitted (which is true, of course), but that didn't mean we didn't suffer from the same maladies as other readers: boredom, short attention spans, a desire to be entertained. Believe me, when I would get to essay number 87 out of 115 on Ben Franklin's autobiography, a paper that got all the facts wrong but offered them entertainingly began to look pretty appealing. Being amusing, however, is not the whole deal with the care and feeding of an audience. There is the small matter of shepherding the reader from the front of the essay to the back, helping them out when they need it with things like explanations and examples, leaving them with the sense of a satisfying experience.

That's not too much to ask, is it?

Over the years, I developed a set of precepts and practices for writing papers for my literature classes, the chief of which had to do with audience:

Write your essay for another student in the class. I mean that literally. Which student is up to you.

What are the implications of writing for a fellow student?

1. You know your audience and understand their state of knowledge and familiarity with the material. You do not retell the story because they've read it.
2. You understand the questions they are likely to have and doubts they may express, and can anticipate where you need to explain or support things.
3. You recognize their boredom threshold and realize you have to be interesting and informative.
4. You have a sense of one person (you) speaking to another.

At this juncture, we would usually walk through these items. In an ideal world—that is, with ideal human beings in it—we might have taken photos of the target student, but in this world that would be creepy and fraught with perils, not least the hard feelings with either being selected by too many classmates or being completely overlooked. So instead, I simply instructed them to form a distinct image of the person they selected. To be clear, no one was ever required to read the final product, but the idea was to guide the composition of the work, not to burden fellow sufferers.

From there, we went forward point by point. What did it mean, for instance, that the reader would have approximately the same state of knowledge as the writer? Someone would offer the certainty that they had read the book. How many times, I would ask, which drew an uncomfortable silence that I usually broke by holding up my index finger. An undergraduate who is not writing on a particular work will read it precisely once, assuming he is diligent. There is no time for rereading in most students' schedules. And because they have read it once, you don't need to retell the story. You will, on the other hand, have to provide salient details from the text, because shockingly few humans have total recall of their reading. You will also, when you make a claim about the work, have to provide examples because left to their own devices, readers will almost always come up with a detail that seems to undermine your argument. The second point, that the writer knows where fellow students will have questions and problems, is critically important, because anticipating and heading off problems is part of what good writing does. Will this point be confusing? Will they have objections to this argument? Where and why? How can I surmount those objections? If the writer successfully anticipates problems, she will ultimately have fewer of them. Item three, on boredom and attention spans, is really an extension of the previous item, but it warrants its own consideration. Being a student, the writer knows the challenges to time and concentration that confront other students. They also know how long they can hold those readers' attention. I used to say it was about seven minutes, or the time between commercial breaks, but we are in the age of TikTok videos, so seven may be closer to one these days. Let's just say that it is not long, so it behooves us never to linger too long on a single line of questioning.

That final point subsumes everything else, so all we really need to remember is this: **writing is a conversation between two people, a writer and a reader.** Numbers don't matter. Whether the writing in question is a letter to a friend, a newsletter for a club of thirty, or a book that aspires to reach millions, writing is a conversation between two people, a writer and a reader. And contrary to what some people claim, the reader whom the writer seeks to reach is not herself. In his excellent book *On Writing Well*, William Zinsser claims that the writer's main audience is the writer herself. I could not disagree more strongly. We can— maybe—all agree that if the writer doesn't please herself, then the project is lost, but I have read entirely too many pieces of lousy but highly self-satisfied writing. I was in graduate school, briefly, with someone who had decided that good academic writing consisted of impenetrable thickets of words and obscure jargon. No obscurantist French critic was ever more opaque than he. We tried to reason with him, but he was determined that he was right and the rest of us were idiots. The faculty, unfortunately for him, agreed with our view.

That's all fine, but what if I'm not a student writing for others like me?

Then do a bit of thinking. What are these people, my target audience, like? Some possibilities rule themselves out instantly: your readers are not a bunch of ancient Greeks. Your audience is somewhat nearer at hand. In a lot of writing situations, the answer is obvious. If you are writing a newsletter for your condo association, you know these people already. You have a pretty good idea of their interests, varied though they be, and their attitudes, if for no other reason than you've talked to them over time. The same is true if the chore of a eulogy falls to you; the family and friends in attendance are likely your family and friends, and in any case the occasion dictates the kind of language you will use and the stories you will tell. With tasks that are further afield, some research may be required. I have spent a good bit of time over the years reading entries in a volume called *Writer's Market*, a publication that consists largely of venues, including book publishers and magazines or other periodicals, for writing of all sorts. And the one constant in those entries is the injunction to *read the publication before submitting*. Why? Because *The New Yorker* does not really care to receive bits of adolescent hilarity best aimed at *Mad* magazine. Or vice versa. Journals have their own target audiences (and they often tell you what those are in their *WM* entries), and yours needs to match theirs. An article on the joys of manure spreading just may not fly with a magazine aimed at urban sophisticates aged twenty-five to thirty-nine. There are all sorts of considerations to make when imagining your audience: age, gender, region, country, education, interests, political leanings, pretty much anything that can in some way define people. That doesn't mean that what you do with such information is straightforward.

If you write for magazines, you will want to know what sort of person reads a given journal. There are various ways you could find that information. Reading the articles is one of the best, but you might also want to read the advertisements. Let's say you want to write an article on the joys of fly-fishing. Nothing fancy, just the fun of going out on a local pond and plopping rubber spiders in front of nesting bluegills. Which can be a lot of fun, by the way. A fly-fishing specialty magazine (there are several on the market) might seem just the ticket, but hold on. Do the readers of a periodical that advertises $600 graphite fly rods and $400 stocking-foot waders that need $200 wading boots really seem like they will need an introduction to the simpler pleasures? Not unless you can bring a *really* new twist to your piece. Those readers are more likely to want to read about the newest, hottest rod that will make them forget that $600 model or fly-in trips to remote locations in search of rare trout species. Your article would likely fit better with a general interest outdoor magazine or even one that doesn't normally cover fishing and hunting but is always looking to get readers hooked on new activities. Which is cool: you didn't really want to write for those high rollers anyway.

These kinds of audience issues are really advanced-tier concerns. The first thing we need to do is learn to write for the audience we have at hand, which for students will often mean classmates and for others, friends, fellow writing group members, work colleagues, neighbors in the community, or some other close-to-home set of readers. That's good news, because often you know those folks well because you are one of them. The basic questions of background, class, education, and the rest can be readily understood. Better still, you can answer the two basic questions that every writer needs to answer about his or her readers: **Why do they need to know what I am going to tell them (or how can I convince them they need to know)?** and **What do I need to do to make them happy that they read it?** If you can provide those two answers, you're good to go. You have figured out the "thou" part of the equation, and you already managed the "I" portion.

So can I write for an audience that isn't like me?

Of course. It is done all the time. As you learn to handle issues of audience—how fast to release information, when to introduce specifics to support your claims, how to anticipate objections—you can and will move outside your familiar circle and address a wider world. Since at that point you can no longer rely on personal connections, however, you may have to do a bit of research, as with our hypothetical fly-fishing article. Not only that, but many times you may have to address multiple audiences at once. Or your audience may become a less cohesive unit. It can even turn out that you are mistaken about your audience.

A number of years ago, I wrote a book called *How to Read Literature Like a Professor*. At the time, I knew with complete certainty who my audience was, distilled down to a single figure: a thirty-seven-year-old, divorced nurse returning to college because licensing rules had changed, and she had decided that this time she wanted to follow her heart and study literature. I know what you're thinking: *this guy is nuts*. That may be, but my position was rational and backed by facts: I had met this person over and over in my classes, the displaced worker beginning a new life. The mostly male version was the former General Motors line worker whose job and maybe entire factory had been shut down. If you taught in Flint, Michigan, during the 1980s and 1990s, you got that story a lot. These were people who had always liked to read but felt that somehow they had been absent the day this mysterious thing, symbolism, was discussed. But they weren't absent and they weren't slackers. They were taught by men and women who did their best but may have had their own issues with not just symbols but figurative thinking generally, the ways in which one thing can be itself literally and something else on another level of the story or poem. Rain can actually be rain but also stand for a kind of cleansing, for instance.

That's who I wrote for, and I found a number of them, some of whom wrote in gratitude for the insights. It turned out, though, that I caught the eyes of others, some of whom had degrees in English and even a certain number of high school English teachers who began inflicting the book on their students, particularly in Advanced Placement classes. I had been writing for a thirty-seven-year-old and landed another audience of seventeen-year-olds. Who knew? Clearly not me. As a consequence, there were small things in the book that came to seem less well-suited to its readers. Not the overall approach, since I had written for grown-ups and I always talk to high schoolers as grown-ups. It's just that some items, mostly throwaway lines and asides, were a little too grown-up. The revised version has even fewer mentions of adult beverages, which were not numerous in any case. **Writing, like life, is adjustment.**

Sometimes, writers know that their readers will not have a direct connection to their subjects—or to the writers themselves. Michelle Obama understood, for instance, that not every reader was going to be a liberal woman of color. The goal was to appeal to as broad an audience as possible as she told her rather improbable story of the road to the White House. Politics being what they are (and whether they care for that fact or not, First Ladies are caught up in politics), there were a lot of people who would reject any book by her without looking at it. But she needed a strategy that could win over open-minded readers who were not attracted by her husband's policies. Her narrative strategy involved candor, sincerity, and openness, the qualities for which she was known while living at 1600 Pennsylvania Avenue and which sometimes landed her in hot water with the political commentariat. After all, Penguin Random House paid gigantic advances for books from the former First Couple, and publishing companies stay in business by turning profits, so all parties were interested in the widest possible readership. It worked: in 2018, a year filled with big, noisy books about President Donald Trump, hers was the bestselling book by or about a political figure. Indeed, despite not coming out until mid-November, it was the top-selling *book* of 2018, period.

That's great, but I don't want to write a bestseller. I just want to write an opinion piece for my local paper.

The principle still holds. If you want to reach fourteen million readers, as *Becoming* had within two years of publication, or a few hundred—or six—you need to understand who is on the other end of your I–thou relationship as well as how best to reach them through words. And never forget, reading is a private experience, as solitary in its way as writing is. **However large your audience, you only reach them one reader at a time.** The measure of success for a writer should be not the size of an audience but the impact of the words in the mind of one reader. Bestsellers are built on the strength of single readers. A big name or wagonloads of hype can move a lot of copies in the first week of a book's release, but titles remain on the list week after week because those early readers tell friends that the books are worth plunking down enough money to buy several days' worth of mocha lattes. Here's the secret of publishing success: sell one copy, repeat.

I get that, but how does knowing my audience affect what I do?

That colors everything you do. As you have surmised, just knowing your audience is a beginning, not an end. Once your readers have been identified, they become the sun at the center of your solar system. Every choice you make is governed by the gravity they exert on your enterprise. Let's say that you are writing an article for fourth graders. Your vocabulary list will be reduced; it will likely not include, for instance, "surmised." You will have to explain some topics that you could assume adult readers know but that nine- and ten-year-olds will not. You will use shorter, simpler sentences than you might for an older readership. You will write, in other words, in the manner of the old *Weekly Reader* (now *Scholastic News/Weekly Reader*), which you may have read in an earlier version of you and which existed for over eighty years by perfectly understanding elementary school readers. This is not to suggest that you condescend or talk down to these young readers (which is never a good plan whatever the audience's age). You strive, rather, to write at a level appropriate for readers' ages and experience.

Take the earlier article on fly-fishing for bluegills, which you are writing for a general audience looking for more outdoor activities. During the 2020 coronavirus shutdown such articles became a staple in newspapers and general interest magazines: here's something you haven't tried but it will add variety to your life and is a lot of fun! The first thing you have to recognize is that your readers will, on average, know nothing about fly-casting. Only two types of humans know anything practical about casting a virtually weightless lure with a line heavy enough to get that little nothing to land somewhere other than at your feet: those who actually fish with flies and those who tried it once or twice and gave it up. For all their differences, those two groups share one property. Neither of those will be your target audience. You're looking to reach those who don't love fly-fishing but haven't decided to despise it. Nor will you want to overburden your readers with details. Your readers need to grasp the sport conceptually and even vaguely, not to pass an exam on the subject. Your tone and handling will be breezy and light (because this activity is fun! fun! fun!). If readers are hooked, they will go off and read some more on the subject.

This book will not, for the most part, deal with specific genres and forms of nonfiction writing. There is, however, one specific type of writing that is still new on the landscape: writing for on-line venues. In the course of my research, I read about a gazillion articles on writing for the web, and they all said almost exactly the same thing, which came down to this: when you write for online spaces, forget almost everything you know about writing. Instead, you have to write for an audience that has an attention span barely longer than that of gnats. You know it's true. I know it's true of me. Reading on a screen is one long parade of distractions that look more interesting than what we set out to do.

That insight bears repeating: **forget *almost* everything you know about writing**. The individual pieces of advice revolve around the theme of brevity: short sentences, short paragraphs, plenty of white space breaking things up, information front-loaded because (as some experts assert) only twenty percent of web-writing will be read. It all sounds a little like modern tele-graphese, the short bursts of prose ("ARRIVED LIVERPOOL STOP SEEKING SUSPECT STOP") that could be rendered in Morse code during an earlier information revolution.

But here's the thing: all that advice follows naturally from the point we've been discussing here, namely that you have to write with your audience in mind. And by audience, we mean not only individual persons but those persons in a specific cultural context. Their expectations would be different if they were reading a book or magazine. But this is a listicle, that odd amalgam of "list" and "article" that satisfies the criteria of neither of the parent forms, and readers have developed their own criteria for judging this new thing.

Whatever your subject, your publishing venue, your reason for writing, one constant remains: you are trying to reach some person who *is not you*. And above all, you want him or her to feel grateful for what you have had to say, for the knowledge you have imparted, for the viewpoint you have shared. Even if readers don't agree with you (and they won't, in the case, say, of a letter of complaint), you still want to part on good terms professionally. When you write for any kind of public consumption, meaning pretty much anything other than diary or journal entries, you want to do justice to both the "I" and the "thou" in this sacred compact of two minds meeting each other.

3

Writing as Exploration of Self

*To be yourself in a world that is constantly trying to
make you something else is the greatest accomplishment.*
—RALPH WALDO EMERSON

A VERY LONG TIME ago when the world was young, I wrote a
research paper for my senior seminar on Charles Dickens with a
title on the order of "Escape Themes in *Our Mutual Friend.*" I was
under the sway of a literary critic you've never heard of who practiced first one and then another school of criticism, which, even
if you had heard of them, wouldn't make any more sense to you
than they do to me, so we'll skip that part. But where that person
comes into play in my psychodrama is that he showed me that if
you concentrated on the particulars of a text, a general pattern
might emerge. And he did so by emphasizing occasions of entrap-
ment, incarceration, and confinement in various of Dickens's late
novels. Ever the literary magpie, I decided that if confinement was
a concern, there must be some occasions of escape, so I explored
the last of Dickens's novels, and sure enough, there they were.

In itself, this insight is somewhere south of brilliant: someone in all those novels is always going to jail or debtor's prison (as the young Charles's father had) or regular prison, and sometimes they narrowly escaped such harrowing outcomes. However inspired or otherwise, the paper turned out to be the best thing I had written all term, confirmed by my professor, who was no pushover, but that's not the point.

This is: I surprised myself.

The plan wasn't startling; I had that from the get-go. It's hard to write an essay without a plan, and for a longer essay (which this was), a firmer plan. Otherwise, your wheels slip in sand and you pitch headlong into the ditch, which the best authorities agree is bad. No, the big reveal wasn't the design but the discovery. It turns out that J. Hillis Miller (the famous critic in question) was not the impetus for writing my essay but merely the nudge to do something I was always going to do. The examples came so fast and insistent that I could hardly keep up. Don't get me wrong— putting the thing together and coming up with the analysis was as difficult as ever—but finding instances that supported my thesis was nearly automatic. In other words, I had been collecting this information the entire time (and it was considerable on a book only slightly shorter than the *Encyclopedia Britannica*). I simply didn't know it.

Writing that essay helped me discover not only what I thought but *how* I thought. There was this unacknowledged—what, habit? instinct? tendency?—in my reading to seek out certain cues having to do with frustration, limitations, and imprisonment that had needed to be explored. So explore it I did. A few years later, when I began teaching James Joyce's story collection, *Dubliners*, I was drawn to the many images of physical barriers such as gates, stiles, fences, locked doors, and even windows. That became one of the entry points for class discussion. At least this time, I recognized the source because I had already been there.

Every piece of writing is an occasion for increasing self-knowledge. We may learn that we can do something we hadn't considered before or that we have an unexpected weak spot. Or that we have a hard time cutting our prose to the bone, or else find ourselves unwilling to fully flesh out ideas. We may surprise ourselves with what we say, for good or ill. The journalist-memoirist Joan Didion expresses that thought in envy-inspiring clarity: "I write entirely to find out what I'm thinking, what I'm looking at, what I see and what it means. What I want and what I fear." I would push slightly beyond that and say that through writing we find out not merely what we think but how we think, but we can only get there once we become comfortable with the act itself.

This revelation doesn't mean that your writing has to be autobiographical, nor that all of your writing is disguised autobiography. As my opening example shows, we can learn about ourselves through almost any sort of written task. I had a friend in grad school who announced one day that she had completed the first draft of her dissertation chapter on *Jane Eyre*. When finished, she said, it would be about twenty-five pages. And how long, I asked, was the current iteration? One hundred and twenty-five pages. I nearly fell over. That was simply her process, she said (apparently my poker face needed work). Her first drafts were always massively overwritten and included pretty much every thought she had or believed she might have later on, so her revision and rewriting were not so much pruning the text as clear-cutting an entire hillside.

I was no more likely to do that than I was to cut off my writing hand. At the shoulder. But she had learned from experience that this method was her best path to good work, and she undertook it quite cheerfully. This sort of realization is something that every writer comes to through experience, and it is one sort of self-discovery. Nonwriters often say to me, "I don't know how someone can write a book." What I think to myself is, it helps to be an egomaniac, but what I tell them is once you learn to write a chapter, which is to say an essay of a given length, you simply string a certain number of them together and arrive at a booklike object. It's easy. Naturally, it is a bit more involved. You have to make those chapters cohere around a subject and to cause them to become (or seem) a mechanism that moves forward as a single entity and not a mere collection of parts. But the principle is simple enough: **learn to write the pieces and then move on to some suitable arrangement of those pieces**. Most dissertations are collections of seminar-paper-length chapters, and doctoral students have spent the previous several years mastering that particular form. In fact, most of the chapters of my dissertation *were* seminar papers, or at least had their first iteration as such, before being harnessed to a single vision of my topic, which governed how they were repurposed and rewritten. Here's a handy rule for writers: **waste not, want not**. If you work hard to perfect a piece of writing, see if it can't do some good in the world, or at the very least, shop it around until you know that it can't find a home. One of my dissertation committee members often told her students that she had published every seminar paper she wrote in graduate school. When you realize that number would only be fifteen to eighteen papers, it isn't quite as amazing as it sounds at first, but it is still pretty darned impressive. Most of us discovered that our publication total for seminar papers was lower. Much lower.

At the same time, every piece of writing is an occasion for self-delusion. I have completed short stories, a novel, academic articles, numerous nonfiction book proposals, and a couple of actual books, each, like Mary Poppins, practically perfect in every way. That's how they felt when I finished them. Somehow, though, history proved otherwise. And by "history," I mean editors, those efficient adjusters of overly enthusiastic self-appraisals. Some of those items listed here were mildly terrible, others just so-so, still others not right for a publishing venue I had deemed ideal. In most cases, the delusion was my own, but in the case of a couple of the books, editors and various members of the publishing house went down the rabbit hole right beside me. We were sure that the books were great, that the world had been waiting for just that item, and that it would sell like snow cones in Death Valley. The greatness of the titles in question was never conclusively disproved, but items two and three in that list suggest an answer in the negative. One book *might* have been a victim of poor timing, since another book along the same lines and from a better-known writer came out just ahead of mine, but the other has no such built-in excuse; it just didn't sell. Every last one of those projects consumed me for somewhere between a week or two and a couple of years. Seeing them go down in flames really hurt. But there is not one that I regret working on. They may not have been efforts the world needed to see, but they were things I needed to do—for reasons of development, for pure intellectual pursuit, for the lessons that failure can teach that might help with future success, for the fun I had in writing them, for what I learned about myself. I was wrong, but I got something positive out of each endeavor, if not the thing I had hoped for.

A different writer might have a different response to such a catalog of failure. It took me a long time to see that failure is a necessary component to success, at least for this writer. Make no mistake, it was frustrating and occasionally crushing to see my labors come to so little. After my first trade book, *How to Read Literature Like a Professor*, came out in 2003, I wanted to do something else, worried that another book in that vein might typecast me as whatever I had made myself into with that first one (my shorthand was the funny-reading-guy, but that might have been giving my humor too much credit). My editor and I went back and forth on this point. I wrote at least five complete proposals for books that used some other part of my talents, and they all came back dead on arrival (but stated nicely). Finally, I agreed to write another like the first, this time with the fourth word changed to *Novels*. As soon as I began it, I wondered why I had resisted. The answer was easy: self-delusion. I felt that I should be doing something else, not that I would be better at something else. That book came out in 2008 but could have happened sooner had I not been a knothead.

In his autobiography, Benjamin Franklin calls an error of this type—a mistake from being too full of oneself—an erratum (the plural of which is errata), meaning an error made in printing a book. Technically, the erratum is the correction issued as a slip of paper carrying the corrected text that is slid between pages or bound into the back of the book. Errata are not criminal but may bring embarrassment when we look back on them. He also sees them as occasions to learn something, which is just like him. And so they are. But only if we choose to learn from them. They can also be paralyzing forces if we get all bound up in fighting them.

Your errata, if any, will be different from mine, and I hope they will include a couple of doozies. I've learned the most from those.

Here is an admirable piece of self-knowledge. Barry Lopez, a great writer of fiction and nonfiction about the natural world, or rather of humans in the natural world, died on Christmas Day 2020. Naturally, there were remembrances and appreciations in all the major media outlets, among them on National Public Radio's *Fresh Air*, which replayed a couple of long interviews, one from 1989 that covered his recent work, including *Arctic Dreams* (1986), which won the National Book Award. During the interview, he said that he didn't think the reader was interested in abstract notions or political or environmental implications. "The reader only wants one thing—the reader wants a wonderful story. And if you can't tell the reader a wonderful story, then you're not writing." This is not an immutable truth for all writers at all times. This is a Barry Lopez truth. Lopez, you see, was a narrative writer. A great many writers are narrative specialists, but there are also those who are essentially argumentative writers or analytical writers or expository writers or informational writers. To be sure, all of those will make use of narrative in their work; the human mind, after all, is geared to process stories. But that is not their main stock-in-trade. But for Lopez, story is everything, and he is very, very good at it. I don't know if he understood it as a personal truth, but it was, and as such it was just what he needed to know.

One of the things that you will learn about yourself in writing—in fact, you can't avoid it and shouldn't want to—is who you are as a stylist. When we hear about prose stylists, we tend to think of those writers whose style is flamboyant, over-the-top: Faulkner or

Hemingway or Toni Morrison or Gabriel García Márquez. Fair enough. They are most definitely stylists. So are you, or at least you will be when you settle into something that is comfortable and natural-feeling, if not entirely natural. Almost all writers flail around for a while, first trying just to put one word after another and then to make them sound the way they believe some other party (readers, instructor, the author of their writing text) expects them to sound.

Forget them! Let's go back to first principles here, or at least the first principle that matters: know thyself. For any passage in your writing, ask yourself, Does this sound *good*? Does this sound good *to me*? Here's the tricky part: you have to answer honestly. Most people, when they hear that caveat, assume that it means, don't let yourself off the hook too easily: "Yeah, that doesn't sound too bad. It'll do." It can certainly mean that you don't settle for "sounding good" because it's off your plate but instead demand that it sound genuinely good. But it can also mean: it doesn't sound good to me because it doesn't sound like [insert favorite writer here]. Here's where we need to admit that we are never going to sound like that special writer, whether it's Kurt Vonnegut or Kurt Cobain, because we are not them. If we try, really try, we will still fail because the result won't sound genuine; it will not be *of* us. I am an accomplished literary mimic. With a bit of study, I can write *like* nearly anyone. As any number of hoaxers have proven, it isn't that hard to bury a page or two in a writer's archive, go back and "discover" it, and claim it as genuine. Often, the forgers are undone by technical details such as the content of the paper or the aging of the ink. Yet in almost every case, someone with great experience of the original writer's oeuvre has cast doubt on the authenticity. Melissa McCarthy starred as forger Lee

Israel in *Can You Ever Forgive Me?* (2018), which captured the elation and despair of that most dubious of literary endeavors. In the film, she experienced success in *sounding* like other writers, but she failed on two counts: she emulated but never truly *inhabited* them, and she never sounded like herself. That's not something to want for yourself; neither was the prison sentence.

Even if one is not copying another writer's style with an intent to deceive, such effort is morally problematic, more for its effect on the later writer than on the original. To deny one's own style in favor of some other author's is to deny an essential part of oneself. It is crucial that we embrace ourselves as writers, whatever our perceived deficiencies. You don't like what you sound like? Improve your sound. Work on your style. Expand your vocabulary. Gain greater mastery of your voice. That may well involve trying on various strategies to see how they fit, which is fine. Learning from other writers is quite different from copying one of them in their totality. I firmly believe that all writing is connected, that every piece of "literature" grows out of and speaks back to every other piece, even if we haven't read all of it—which no one ever has. We use lessons we have learned, talk back to writers we admire and others we detest, enter into conversations not only with the writers we have read but with those they had read and so on back through time. That is not the same, however, as slavishly following the example of a single writer. We had our Mark Twain, our Jane Austen, and don't need another. In his creative writing text, *Three Genres: The Writing of Poetry, Fiction, and Drama* (1965), Stephen Minot addressed a phenomenon not unknown to teachers of fiction writing: "Mock Faulkner." What he was describing was a certain sort of student (male, in this case) who went all-in on his favorite author and produced enough mayhem for an entire

Faulkner novel in six or seven pages, the whole thing taking place in a Mississippi wilderness of tangled prose. Every creative writing teacher has seen some variant of this sort of fanboy-or-girl story. It does not produce good fiction. Or good style.

You know what does? Honest writing in which the creators know themselves, both assets and liabilities, and produce prose that is personal and at the same time welcoming to readers. Or, if not exactly welcoming, strong in ways that will justify its difficulty. You may not be able to produce Faulkner—and please don't—but you can absolutely write the way I just suggested. By being true to yourself, you create a style and forms that are strong and can become stronger as you become more assured. That's something we all would like to read.

4

Writing as Exploration of Subject

Writing is a way to explore a question and gain control over it.
—WILLIAM ZINSSER

A COLLEAGUE ONCE SAID to me that he had spent the previous evening reading a poem by a writer of some renown. I asked if it was a long one. "No," he said, "only about a page long, but for me to really understand a poem takes an entire evening." This led to a discussion of why and how we attack poems when we really want to know not only what they have to say but how they go about saying it, and I came away thinking that his estimate sounded about right.

For my part, the only ways I have ever really grown to know a lyric poem, whether sonnet or free verse, are to teach it and to write about it. Of the two, writing is by far the surest path. Nor does the subject have to be literary. The act of writing forces an examination of the subject through research, analysis, and expression, whether the topic is physics or phys ed. There was a survey analysis course in college in which the statistical side of things made no sense to me at all—until I was made to write about the findings. Understand, I got plenty wrong in writing about it, but even the errors made me understand the material better. When we write about subjects, that act brings a human intelligence into contact with a new knowledge base, and in wrestling with it, we create our thoughts about that knowledge.

It was not always so. When I was learning to write for academic purposes, I had to concentrate so hard on not screwing up that my focus was on the process, not the subject: How many sentences here or there, what order of supporting evidence, what sort of thesis sentence, what have I forgotten? None of this is because my teachers were especially harsh or because the forms they were teaching were so difficult to master. The difficulty, instead, was that the entire business was external to me. So, then the question becomes: Why was it such an alien process? Rules. Unlike the ideas I might have about a subject, which were generated from the inside, everything about the *process* of committing them to paper seemed to come from some foreign entity, from an inscrutable and not very compassionate god: "Put it here! No, not there! Do it this way! Use that other word! Have X number of sentences in your paragraph!" For whatever reason, this high-handed deity was devoted to exclaiming.

Okay, some of my alienation from the activity might have had to do with the subject matter seeming foreign, as with that survey analysis course. All those statistical terms! But even when I was writing on subjects with which I was more conversant, I was not conversing all that well on paper. Eventually, though, the pieces came together, more or less. I found that writing introductions, for example, became less unnatural by dint of sheer practice. Then, curiously, that if my introduction was good enough, it dictated where the rest of the paper needed to go. Or at least, up until the conclusion; those remained mysterious for rather longer. What happened, I believe, is that two things occurred. First, I internalized the rules to the point that I could stop thinking about them and focus on the subject. The second is that as I became better at immersing myself in the subject, I worried less about whether I was doing it *right*.

Here's a thought. Let's cut out the middle-person. Or middle-deity, the one with all the exclamation marks. How? By putting the emphasis on the learner, on using writing to understand subjects, ideas, arguments more fully. And secondly, of course, on the reader, if different from the learner.

It is not inevitable that all writing must have a reader, at least not the external sort. There are many forms of writing that are entirely private, even when the writing is about difficult subjects. You might not write in your diary about survey analysis or *Great Expectations*, unless you imagine your diary as part of your literary estate (think Virginia Woolf here), but you might keep a *reading journal* where you work through ideas and issues. A reading journal, unlike a diary, has a specific intellectual or educational function: it should help you collect your thoughts, questions, and critiques of what you read. We tend to think of reading journals as things to keep, under duress, in literature classes. After all, where else is there so much reading? Philosophy courses spring to mind, along with history, sociology, political science, pretty much anything in the humanities and social sciences. The hard sciences might have less reading in terms of volume, but assignments can make up in difficulty what they lack in length. For that matter, I once took a physics course that was as much philosophy and religion as it was velocity and gravitation. The reading list included two books by Albert Einstein, whose mind ranged quite far from his most famous equation. Even if you are not in school, your reading journal can record what you think as you read as well as what the books actually say. I will admit that I have never been a journal keeper, in part because my method of note taking as I read is quite extensive; I often wind up with a whole sheaf of papers that do what a journal might do, only in a more cryptic fashion and with terrible printing. Handwriting died for me long years ago, and even ball-and-stick printing is sometimes a challenge, so journaling holds little personal appeal, although it works for any number of my colleagues.

The question arises at this point as to what we mean by "writing about it." Is jotting in the margins sufficient? If so, does one jot on a test tube? Or on a cosmological theory? What about a journal entry? Will that do? Is an essay required? How about a letter? Email? Text message? That is up to you, although I will say that you need to give yourself enough room to figure things out, so maybe text messages are inadequate. To decide what form is best for you, we need to understand what this written interaction is and what we want it to accomplish. Here is how I would characterize the act: a three-sided conversation among the writer, the source material, and some real or imagined audience (which may or may not simply be the writer's future self). The purpose of this sort of exercise is to figure out what the writer thinks (or feels, because that also matters) about the subject of the writing and, at least as important, why he or she thinks or feels that way.

What forms can that trilateral discussion take? Just about anything you can envision.

Review. One approach is to write a review. The world is full of reviews of books, movies, television programs, podcasts, and pretty much anything else in the realm of human communication. But you can also review ideas, information, whole subjects. After all, book reviews are written about nonfiction books on subjects like geology, anthropology, and the origins of the universe as well as about novels about wizards trapped in werewolf colonies. There are two essential parts of a review: the writer's response and the examination of the "text" (print or visual or auditory, for instance) that prompts that response. If the reviewer finds this poetry volume less compelling than the poet's last collection, he owes it to readers—and to the poet under consideration—to explain why that verdict is justified. It isn't really enough to simply say, "I thought this book sucked"; you have to identify the source of its suckiness. The point of this exercise (unless you hope to publish your review, in which case that is the point) is to put you in touch with your intellectual/emotional response system. Why do you react to this information the way you do? What is it telling you about yourself? Beyond that, what can you learn about the source material from careful examination of your reactions? What was in it that you found comforting or disquieting or infuriating? This is not an approach you would want to take with all material (none of them likely is), but in the right situations, it can be valuable.

Explication. In my experience, complicated material is impossible to explain to someone else if I don't understand it myself. The best way to gain that understanding? Write it out. That act of writing will let you see the things that you do grasp while at the same time forcing you to admit that there are parts about which you have no clue. Best of all, the realization forces you to get a handle on what you didn't get the first time (or any handle at all). You can't very well explain the concepts or data or whatever the hang-up is (and "explicate" is just a two-dollar word for "explain") until you can actually make sense of them. In the matter of audience for explications, you have some choices. You can, for instance, write for someone who is at roughly your knowledge level on the subject, taking as a given that your readers will struggle where you have and benefit from your having worked through your problems. Be advised, though: you cannot slide over the tough bits. Be honest with yourself. If something is beyond you, say so. Put it in its own paragraph so you can find it when the light finally goes on. Just don't skip over it as if everything is copacetic. Deluding yourself is not useful. So what if you admit failure on some difficult concept? No one's reading it but you.

Analysis. Take the item under study apart and see how it works. Analysis is the basis for most advanced study. In the primary and middle grades, students are given information to be internalized. It is hard to undertake more elevated study of mathematics if one has to stop and work out the product of four times four. In high school, a great deal of internalization—which we think of as memorization, because that's what we had to do to internalize information—still takes place, but teachers begin to emphasize analytical skills. Simply knowing facts stops being sufficient, and arranging them in ways that help tell the story behind them becomes more important. That process becomes more crucial at each stage of education from then on. Does the Gettysburg Address really say what we think it does on first reading? What were the consequences of the Missouri Compromise, and were they inevitable or avoidable? What should we make of Frost's word choices in "The Road Not Taken"?

Op-ed. Judging from social media, everyone has something to get off their chests. Every. Single. Minute. Of. The. Day. Sorry, lapsed into Facebook mode there. Still, the evidence does suggest that as a people we are fired up, enthusiastic, outraged, even more outraged, inspired, deluded, and passionate, in no particular order. Something has moved a great many people to post their opinions irrespective of facts so that other people can read them. Often, those opinions are couched in language that is barely recognizable as belonging to any linguistic family, certainly not one that adheres to punctuation, sentence structure (or even existence), and other niceties that make them readable by actual people. The very nature of social media platforms works against the pursuit of ideas, of rational discussion of issues, of thought. Facebook, for instance, rewards the ability to attract eyeballs (an unappealing image, but that's the language used). Well, what attracts attention? Terseness, punchy delivery, snark, brevity. Twitter actively enforces them, particularly the last one. Even the comparatively generous 280-character limit, double the original, doesn't allow for explanations or nuance. That's just as well, because the audience, in my experience, has no patience for such things. In a majority of cases, commentators respond not to content but to the title of a post; it astonishes me how many people feel the need to reply without ever reading the post. Even truth doesn't matter, only how strong the punch you throw lands. And make no mistake, truth has been a casualty of our fondness for brevity.

We can, just maybe, do better. Better for ourselves, if no one else. Who knows? Bettering ourselves might even prove salutary for the larger society. When you feel really strongly about some item in the news, some Supreme Court decision, some verbal outrage by a legislator or television talking head, try something different. Write about it. Really write, not just fire off some half-baked comment on your chosen platform.

That sounds like work. What would I get that makes it worth the labor?

True, there is some work involved. The argument that the labor itself produces value is beyond us these days, but I think there is value in work, that it builds some needed quality in us. If that's all too myth-of-Sisyphus-existentialist for you, so be it. I'll push the rock up that hill on my own. There are other values. For one thing, in digging into a controversy in enough depth to produce writing, we are forced to understand it better than our prior casual acquaintance with it permitted. Another benefit is that we learn our own minds better. Why do we hold the view that we do? How does it turn out to be related to the facts of the matter? Have we been forced to adjust our views? How and why? Those reasons ought to suffice to get you started.

Before we start, however, there are definitions to attend to. First, what is an op-ed, anyway? From the look of it, you might be tempted to believe, as I once did, that it is a conjoining of "opinion" and "editorial." So close, and yet . . . You see, in newspaper parlance, "editorial" refers to something written by the staff of the paper itself, while "opinion" refers to commentary written by anyone not a staffer. In fact, the "ed" part of "op-ed" refers to editorials, but the "op" portion indicates that the commentary appears *opposite* the *editorial* page. Back in the golden age, or dark ages (depending on how old you are and how and even if you remember that era) when even small-market newspapers ran two pages of commentary, the editorials appeared on the *verso* (meaning "left"), or left-of-the-center page, while the *recto* (meaning "right") appeared on the right-hand side. Why not just "left" and "right" or "front" and "back," since every recto has its verso on the back side? Because those words have other uses. The front and back pages refer to the first and last pages of a section, while right and left can refer, among other things, to columns on a given page. Meanwhile, Latin, being a dead language, had these words, *recto* and *verso*, just lying around not earning their keep, so newsmen (and they were men, for better and worse, when all this began) snapped them up.

And then there is the matter of "opinion." I won't claim that it has been more degraded than any other English word, but few words have suffered degradation that has been more culturally disastrous. At one time, that word meant something like "a judgment or viewpoint that, while not a statement of fact, is informed by knowledge." Now, too often, it means merely "this is my knee-jerk reaction to something I don't understand." We all have such reactions, but are they worth sending out into the world if they have no basis in reality other than our own prejudices? In fact, there is a logical fallacy embedded in that sort of definition that "I have a right to my opinion." Australian philosopher Patrick Stokes has argued persuasively that such a strategy is meant to cut off discussion when arguing from a factually inferior position, implying as it does "an equal right to be heard on a matter in which only one of the two parties has the relevant expertise." In other words, expert opinion and uninformed opinion are not equivalent, which may be why various factions in contemporary society spend so much time trying to discredit expertise or knowledge. The idea that all opinions are equally valuable, let alone that ones not based in knowledge are somehow superior, is fatuous at best and malicious at worst. So let us aim in our opinion pieces, our commentaries, to use real knowledge, real data, and real facts.

So, you have a burning issue and a vision about it. Maybe it is about the value of nongovernmental charities that help the poor.

Maybe it is about how shipping grapes from Chile in wintertime is a terrible misuse of fossil fuels. With either of these, there are numerous studies that can help you craft your commentary. You do not have to agree with them, but you should be prepared to defend your position. This need to support and defend one's views is a traditional expectation regarding opinion pieces. It is not enough simply to reject or demean another position or set of facts simply based on whim. If you read a number of national opinion columnists, you will quickly discover that they are aware of this expectation. Most adhere to the demands; a few try to skirt them with fancy footwork so no one notices, which you will quickly spot once you are aware of the rules of the road. As with all these writing projects, how much you decide to follow the rules for the form when out in public depends on whether you intend for your piece to be public. If it's entirely private, you can do whatever you want with no worries about reception. If, on the other hand, you think you might want to place your commentary in the local paper, then audience expectations become a much greater concern. You will want better quality sources than you might demand of yourself, stronger logic if there is someone else to convince, more accurate data if called for. In other words, you will probably want to clean up your act.

Every type of writing has different expectations from every other, as well as a host of shared ones. Opinion and commentary fall into the category of *persuasive* writing along with such things as editorials and arguments. On one level, all nonfiction is persuasive writing in that writers are trying to convince or persuade readers to read what they are offering. Writing that is intended to convince, on the other hand, has more specific requirements. The writer must lay out claims, back them up with facts, and somehow pin them together. Those elements are, in fact, the main three in what is known as the Toulmin model of argument. In his 1958 book, *The Uses of Argument*, British philosopher and professor Stephen Toulmin laid out six principles to follow in constructing a successful argument. The first three are *claim*, *grounds*, and *warrant*. The claim is simple enough to understand: it is the assertion the writer makes to establish the goals of the argument. Let's say that in conversation a friend tells you that she wasn't born in any state but has been a United States citizen from birth. That's her *claim*. You're skeptical, so you challenge her claim. She responds that she was born in Guam, which is an American territory. This is her *ground*. Still unconvinced, you ask for explanation. Your friend points out that the fourteenth amendment to the Constitution guarantees birthright citizenship for all persons born in the United States, including its incorporated territories. That is her *warrant*, the thing that pins claim to ground. You apologize for doubting her, accept her claim as valid, and swear to yourself that you really need to read the Constitution sometime.

That, in effect, is your charge in writing your opinion piece. You must make your claim, your main point of the argument, then buttress it with grounds (and more than one is usually helpful), and then establish their relation to one another by the warrant. Make no mistake, all the usual duties of public writing also obtain. You must be clear, must proceed in an orderly fashion, must anticipate the readers' doubts and challenges, must adduce supporting facts and statements, must construct a winning opening and a satisfying conclusion. As a laundry list of obligations, this looks quite intimidating. In the event, if you keep in mind your own goals and your readers' needs, it will seem a lot less abstract and a good deal more straightforward.

One of the great things about persuasive writing is that, if undertaken seriously, it advances the *writer's* grasp of the subject. There's nothing like having to make sense of an issue and support your claims with facts and explanations to clarify not just beliefs but knowledge. Hard to beat that.

There are numerous challenges and pleasures you can set for yourself to assist in learning new materials. Here are a very few, offered as examples rather than as assignments in themselves:

- Write a letter to some past author offering praise or criticism. Tell Thoreau that his rationale in *Walden* for refusing to use the newly invented railroad seems flimsy. Explain what you believe he failed to consider. Write to Shakespeare that his plays would be more pleasurable if he included more of his slapstick "clowns" and fewer brooding, doomed heroes.
- Describe a complex painting in massive detail. Make it feel as if you have as many descriptive phrases as the artist has brushstrokes. Do nothing beyond describe; for the moment, that is your only job.
- In an article or chapter on a technical or scientific subject, find a passage that is unclear or confusing (shouldn't be too hard) and rewrite it so that it makes more sense to the common person (this will be hard).
- Find a scene that is down on its luck—a farm whose barn is in bad shape, a storefront business, a factory that has recently closed—and describe it from the vantage point of the owner who has just discovered that his son is com-

ing home from dangerous duty (fighting forest fires or serving in a war). Don't mention the son or the nature of the danger. Merely present a description that captures the mindset of the owner/father.

Take some abstract field of knowledge (almost anything in astronomy or physics will do) and write about what makes the abstraction so difficult for an ordinary person. This will be more challenging if you actually are an astronomer or physicist, so pick a different field.

Again, let me remind you that these exercises are only touching the surface, and they are coming from a mind that has its own limitations. Try them or not. You may look at mine and think, I can do better. And you can. In any case, you will soon be creating your own exercises. Just make sure they stretch your abilities. How? Use your imagination.

How does writing help more than simply thinking about the subject matter? Chiefly, by not allowing us to get away with sloppiness. "Thinking" is a very approximate term. We use it when we are really drilling down for hard-won insights, but also when we only vaguely have ideas (or have only vague ideas). Are those the same things? I'm voting no on that one. Writing can bring those inchoate musings up to the level of real thought if we put in genuine effort. How? Like this:

Precision. We give ourselves a lot of latitude about ideas until we write them down. In writing, that same latitude looks like carelessness. We need to say what we really mean, particularly when we anticipate that someone else might look at that writing someday.

⌒ **Specifics.** In order for writing to make sense, we need to cite chapter-and-verse—quotes, paraphrases, statistics, calculations, whatever the intellectual currency of the discipline under study is. We must get closer to the material than we would any other way except by teaching it. Staying with the broad contours is never enough to write about a subject, which is why writing is a pain as well as why it benefits our understanding.

⌒ **No fudging.** When the supergroup The Traveling Wilburys formed, they took their name from ex-Beatle George Harrison's repeated comment to producer (and future Wilbury) Jeff Lynne, regarding errors created by faulty equipment on his previous solo effort, *Cloud Nine*, that "we'll bury it in the mix." George's Liverpudlian accent being what it was, it came out as "wilbury it," and for some reason that sounded like a band name. Our problem as writers is that there is no mix in which to bury errors. We have to face up to them, fix them, and generally avoid slop.

⌒ **Research.** Oh, stop that. "Research" simply means finding things out, which you do pretty much anytime you write. You think not? Then consider this: looking up a subject on Wikipedia or entering it in a search engine is research. So is asking your mom for that anecdote about your great-aunt Mathilda locking the preacher in the outhouse so you can have your facts straight in her eulogy. We almost always need to know at least a little more about our subject when we begin writing. That's what research is: finding out things we don't know to add to what we do know.

✐ **Shapeliness.** Some lines back I threw the word "inchoate" at you to describe the half-formed, incompletely realized ideas and disordered arrangement that we often pass off as "thinking" about the subject matter we deal with. Alas, there is no opposite word, "choate," to describe the resolution of this irresolute mental process; the word comes to us from the Latin *incohare* with the prefix already affixed. Just as well; people would see it as Choate, the elite boarding school attended by folks like the Kennedys. So we'll have to get by without clever wordplay here. What writing does is to bring shape and substance to what previously was messy and insubstantial. In other words, it imposes something like order on what had been chaos.

Order is important as a goal. If we are going to write about that challenging idea with enough clarity that we can explain it to another person, we have to order our own thoughts and arrange them in a way that causes them to make sense to someone who is not inclined to let us off the hook. Thinking about what readers demand, I believe, is why we need to write for someone outside ourselves, even if we don't intend to show it to that mythical being. On the other hand, if we do show our work to others, understanding readers' psychology stops being theoretical and becomes more interesting and, usually, rewarding. Also slightly terrifying, but that goes away with practice. A little.

I get that, but how do I go about writing on an unfamiliar subject? If it's unfamiliar, that means I never had an assignment in school to get the hang of it.

Tough to argue with that point. You can do this because (a) you have a brain and (b) you know how to use it. Those factors are more valuable than specific knowledge of an academic discipline. Plus, you don't have to pick a subject you know nothing about. Most of my writing has been exactly in my wheelhouse: literature written in the twentieth (and later, twenty-first) century. It is also true, however, that I raised the concept of "unfamiliar" terrain. Here's what I would do to get started. First, understand whatever it is that will be the object of study. Then look for an opening, a crack in what at first seems a solid façade. I don't mean a weak spot in an argument or some artistic failure you can rip, but a path to understanding it from the inside. For a poem, that might be a particular image or a pattern of word usage. Why does this poem that is not about winter nevertheless use wintry imagery (snow, cold, frost, icy winds)? What does it mean in Frost's "The Road Not Taken" that he says the two paths are worn about the same but then says he took the one less traveled by? For a more technical subject, look at what might trip up the casual reader and try to make that clearer or expressed in simpler language. If you're dealing with a work of history or biography, watch for the ways that this work undercuts or upends what "common knowledge" tells us. Most of all, watch for places that resonate with you or frustrate you or seem discordant. In other words, find the spots that make you need to say something.

The bottom line on writing to explore a subject is that the act forces the writer to engage, really engage with the material. It is easy, as well as entirely human, to slough off when we read or hear or otherwise encounter new or difficult material: "Okay, I get it. Moving along . . ." When we make ourselves bear down on that same material, the process is a continuing series of discoveries that we hadn't "got it" at all. Do I write about every poem or novel I read? Absolutely not. The minds in my family do not run to madness. But if I really need to understand a writer or her work, absolutely yes. Or if I want to understand some broader phenomenon in the literary realm. Some years ago, I came across a lot of new novels that were written as a group of stand-alone short stories, with varying degrees of connection between them. That discovery caused an intellectual itch, and before long, I had started an article. If you want to learn new subjects, find your own itch.

5

Writing as a Locus of Play

You can make anything by writing.
—C. S. LEWIS

THROUGHOUT THIS BOOK I emphasize writing with an eye toward the needs of the reader. Such an approach is entirely appropriate. Nearly all writing is undertaken with a public function in mind—to enlighten, to argue, to describe, to narrate—which is why nearly every instructional book on nonfiction focuses on the utilitarian function of such writing. But "nearly all" is not the same as "all." What if the only intended audience is the writer herself? In such a case, why is she writing? What does she seek to accomplish?

I just said that most writing seeks a public hearing, but it is also true that almost all of it grows out of some private curiosity, that intellectual itch I spoke of in the previous chapter. Not all curiosity relates to subject matter. Sometimes we're curious about what we can make a piece of writing do in terms of form or idea arrangement or language. There are ways to gain insight into a fictional character's mind other than inventing stream-of-consciousness writing as James Joyce, William Faulkner, Virginia Woolf, and others did in the front half of the twentieth century. They were tired of the way that their nineteenth-century predecessors depicted the workings of the brain and wanted to explore the latest discoveries in the new science of psychology. They didn't know what the results might be, and they had no models to follow, but they decided to find out on their own. That's why no stream-of-consciousness writer sounds even remotely like any other. They were so many mad scientists working in separate laboratories and achieving separate results. The results can be challenging for readers but also thrilling.

Whatever else it accomplishes, writing frees our minds to go places—intellectually, creatively, and spiritually—that we might never go otherwise. Writing is about more than the subject, more than the viewpoint, more than the assignment or purpose; it is about the writer bringing themselves to bear on a task. It is an act of turning *nothing* into *something*. That act requires whatever the writers are willing to bring of themselves. You can choose to hold back, to protect some aspects of yourself, to not give too much away, but I would advise cutting loose, making your whole being available. At its best, writing is a full-contact activity. Athletes speak of being "in the zone," of moments of mastery when they are almost seeing themselves from the outside, when the game slows down, when the basket is as big as an oil drum, the fastball a pumpkin in slow motion. Writers find zones, too, when their ideas and the ways to express them are so clear that fingers can barely keep up, when what appears on-screen surprises even themselves, when everything is magical. You can get there but not by holding back.

Some of this experimental writing will be public and some meant only for the experimenter. There are all sorts of private writing that we do or might undertake, and the reasons are nearly as many as the people who undertake them. The first item most of us think of is the diary, surely the most private of all forms of writing, right? The books even come with little locks to make sure. Ninety-nine percent of the time that assessment is correct, but in a tiny fraction of cases diarists (quite often literary types) write with an eye to posterity: What will later generations make of this? The English novelist Virginia Woolf was a devoted diarist who, judging from the results, never wrote a word without imagining some eventual reader. When her diaries began appearing in 1979 with the first of five volumes, they were met with wide interest and solid sales. More importantly, they sparked renewed interest in Woolf as a major literary figure. That the timing coincided with second-wave feminism's revaluation of a host of overlooked or underappreciated women artists and thinkers certainly did not hurt, but *The Diary of Virginia Woolf* is a compelling read on its own. Two and a half centuries earlier, Samuel Pepys (pronounced "Peeps"—seriously) kept a diary during one of the most tumultuous decades in English history, 1660–69. Its beginning coincided with the Restoration of the Crown and the coronation of Charles II, and it detailed, along with his personal exploits and affairs, the Great Plague, which killed over one hundred thousand Londoners in 1665, and the Great Fire of London the following year. While the diary is deeply personal, sometimes embarrassingly so, it is split on intent toward outsiders. Pepys did not want his contemporaries to read it, so he wrote it in shorthand and used a sort of code based on other languages, especially when recounting his sexual peccadilloes, although his code is easily broken by his use of English coarse words. But he very much wanted later generations to have access, hence his proudly placing it in his library. That diary provides us with the best street-level view of the great city for any decade in its history. The most important example of the form was written by a girl in her early teens who would never reach her late teens, would never see her book published. Did Anne Frank envision *The Diary of a Young Girl* finding a readership outside herself? Would she have approved of so intimate a picture of life hiding from the Nazis being shared with the world? Alas, we can't know. What we do know is that she wrote it, in the first instance, for an audience of one. The expectation for diarists is rarely for innermost secrets to be broadcast on the winds. Wrestling with the self *for* the self is usually plenty.

Journals, which sound like the same thing as diaries but need not be, are another form of personal writing as routine. A journal (the root word, *jour*, is French for "day") is a regular, even daily, record of some aspect of the writer's experience, the chief difference being that unlike a diary its focus tends to be outward, looking at the world rather than oneself. There are reading journals that focus on books the writer has read or, sometimes, stopped reading; viewing journals for plays or movies or television programs; professional journals kept by, say, businesspeople or diplomats who may go back to those pages for reference when writing their memoirs; observational journals in which the writers speak about events of the day and their reactions to them; and journals attending to just about any subject you can name.

Beyond the realm of daily-life recording, personal writing offers all sorts of options. In the last forty years or so, a newish nonfiction form has sprung up, using the tools of fiction writing to record things that really happened. In other words, it uses the techniques of creative writing—scene setting, point of view, effective use of dialogue, chapter organization, direct presentation of thought, even at times something approaching stream of consciousness—to write about the real world, including how the writer experiences it. It isn't really a new genre, going back to Henry David Thoreau's *Walden*, James Agee's account of southern sharecroppers, with photographs by Walker Evans, *Let Us Now Praise Famous Men*, and Annie Dillard's *Pilgrim at Tinker Creek*, but the naming, along with the sheer volume of production, is recent. Two of those three titles are memoirs, and personal histories loom large in the genre, from childhood reminiscences all the way to the struggles and grief of widowhood in Joan Didion's *The Year of Magical Thinking* (2005) and Joyce Carol Oates's *A Widow's Story* (2011). These examples are all intended to reach an audience, but memoir, or *creative nonfiction* more broadly, can be for your eyes only. Writing about experience is a way to frame it and make it understandable, to give it shape and texture and perspective—because unlike diaries and journals, memoirs afford the luxury of time between events and their telling, whether that time is measured in weeks or decades. You may reach the end of yours and decide that it is so good, that it has so much to offer the world, that you would be remiss not to publish it. Or you may decide that its best home is on your shelf or your hard drive, that it has performed its intended function merely by existing. Either choice is fine, the right to decide belonging to the writer alone.

A word of caution, though: if you intend for your piece to remain private, the only way to ensure that outcome is to take it to the grave with you. Any number of our classics (consider the case of Czech short story writer and novelist Franz Kafka, whose dying wish that his manuscripts be burned was, happily for us, ignored by his friend Max Brod) have survived authorial intentions because of disobedient friends, siblings, and literary executors.

Sometimes, we write privately to purge anger, disgust, or any one of the negative emotions. Publishing the results, even if possible, might make matters worse while bringing no credit to the writer. These pieces often take the form of commentaries, letters to no one, op-eds with no newspaper to receive them. I have spent parts of the last couple of years writing from a place of moral fury. In early 2020, I had a book, *How to Read Nonfiction Like a Professor*, released just as every bookstore in the country shut down. The timing could have been better, as a great many fellow writers can attest. As part of the broader topic of reading nonfiction with greater clarity and understanding, I spent a handful of chapters talking about political discourse, online discussions, social media, and, inevitably, misinformation and the more sinister, deliberate disinformation.

I had no idea what was coming. The COVID-19 pandemic and the 2020 political campaigns were nearly drowned in a sea of misinformation, much of it knowingly false and intended to mislead. Some of it came from foreign actors trying to destabilize the country, although for the majority of it we have no one to blame but ourselves. As that year turned into the next one and I read more and more lies posing as truth about the outcome of the presidential election by the losing candidate and his followers as well as about the seriousness of the pandemic and the efficacy of vaccines, I found myself repeatedly writing ripostes to a lot of phony arguments and invented "facts" and "statistics," all of which ran counter to the known and confirmed truth on both subjects. I had no intention of publishing any of my op-ed writing, nor have I (or will I). Instead, I wrote them for two reasons. First, I had to get all of that off my chest, which I felt would burst if I didn't write it down, so great was my fury at the "Big Lie" about the stolen election and a thousand smaller lies around the same subject or coming from many of the same people. And second, I needed to marshal my arguments on these topics should I find myself called upon to counter falsehoods that I couldn't ignore. I'm not sure whether or not this sort of writing-as-self-defense comes under the rubric of *play*, but it was impossible not to do and intended for no one but me, so I include it. And I suppose this activity was a form of play, since it gave me room to express ideas and emotions freely, without worrying over how they would be received.

Writing for ourselves alone offers the chance to explore forms that might be intimidating or outside our experience or expertise. We might even chance upon a new form, some approach to communication that we have never seen before.

But what if it exists elsewhere and I just don't know about it?

What do you care? You're just doing this for yourself, right? Besides, if you change your mind and want to go public (which is all *publishing* means), there is plenty of time to find out if your new form is all that novel, as well as whether that even matters.

So, what do you want to do with this formal freedom? Maybe write fables Aesop never thought about? Write Socratic dialogues on your own special philosophy? Worked for Plato. Write free verse with idiosyncratic spacing? There's no law against it, especially if the verse is only for you.

Several years ago, I started writing down experiences with nature—odd animal behavior, the blades of wind turbines peeking above a ridge, flowers blooming out of season—that prompted a thought, no matter how small. I had solid historical precedent. Three and a half centuries before, French philosopher and mathematician Blaise Pascal wrote an apologia for Christian belief in the form of short observations and quick, incisive arguments. He called them *Pensées*, "thoughts" in French. He wrote hundreds of them, a great many of which remained unfinished at his death at just thirty-nine. Fast-forward a couple of centuries and English novelist and poet D. H. Lawrence took up the mantle with his collection *Pansies* (1929), published the year before his death at forty-four. His title, the English cognate for Pascal's, was chosen deliberately as an homage and challenge; he, too, wanted to explore and extol his belief system with an even greater emphasis on birds, beasts, and flowers (to use another of his titles) as a springboard to his discussion. Pascal's thoughts were expressed in prose, Lawrence's in free verse.

When I decided to write my own pensées, I chose the original title rather than the translation. And why not? Unlike Lawrence, I had no expectation of publishing the thing, which might turn out to be only a couple of observations. At the time, I only had one experience that I knew I wanted to record: driving across a short bridge in a snow squall when a Cooper's hawk slammed into a male cardinal, creating an explosion of scarlet feathers against a field of white flakes, the whole thing framed by the boundary of my windshield. As soon as it happened, I needed to get home and write it down, although I didn't know why, only that the scene demanded recording. Immediately upon picking up my laptop, a question arose: What form should this tiny narration take? I began in prose, again emulating Pascal, but by the tenth one, they had come to resemble poems of various shapes and arrangements, including one that used three-line unrhymed stanzas with each line indented a few spaces from the one before. Why? It just felt right in some cases. When it didn't, I tried on another form.

Whatever form I selected, I always had some sort of rule about line length or stanza arrangement or even whether lines ended with punctuation or not. With some entries, I used no punctuation at all, making the lines do all the work. This last form I borrowed from a more recent antecedent, W. S. Merwin, who eschewed punctuation in his poems in much of his later work and who only died in 2019 at age ninety-one (proving that nature writing is less harmful to health than the examples of Pascal and Lawrence might suggest). I'm no Merwin (or Lawrence or Pascal), but I know a good model when I see one. Again, why these choices? Why not? The thoughts were mine, so I had every right to express them in whatever form I chose. Besides, they weren't going anywhere other than to take up residence on my hard drive. The question might occur to you: Just what are these things you create? It certainly did to me. I can't call them "prose pieces" because most of them are written in lines. And I have too much respect for the poets of my acquaintance to call them "poems." From my perspective, most of them haven't been worked over enough to bring them to the tightness that proper poems (whether traditional form or free verse) attain. I finally settled on "verselike objects," should anyone ask. To date, no one has. After all, I mostly keep them to myself.

The beauty of this arrangement is that I can horse around with the form, with the arrangement of lines and stanzas, if any, pull them out of lines entirely and turn them back into prose—although the appellation "proselike objects" is clearly nonsense—or introduce any sort of change that occurs to me without considering what the critics might say. There is only one critic, and he's never satisfied, if rarely too demanding.

These instances are hardly the full list of what you can do

to play with language. When I was in fifth grade, a boy named Doug sat behind me in some class that came with plenty of free time to read or do other language-related activities. For a while he and I had contests to see how long we could make sentences that were actually proper sentences and not run-on monstrosities, so we draped our sentences with modifiers and dependent clauses as long as our energy held out. Sometimes Doug's were longer and sometimes mine were, and if we hardly ever reached the holy grail of filling an entire sheet of paper (one side), it was not bad for two youngsters just coming up on their eleventh and twelfth birthdays. That activity won't be everybody's idea of a good time, but it provided us with hours of good, clean, school-approved fun. And maybe we learned something in the process.

Listen, there's no reason you have to undertake any writing just for the sheer pleasure of piddling around with language. If it's not your bag, remember that this is not an assignment book. If, on the other hand, you would like to do more writing where you owe nothing to anyone but yourself, here are a few possibilities. The world is full of others. Write evocative descriptions of buildings that catch your eye. Rewrite passages in newspapers or magazines or books to make them sound better than the originals. Translate technical writing into a more user-friendly version. In other words, do what makes you feel good. You will be more interested in sticking with the activity. When I took piano lessons as a kid, the books were instructional music by François Couperin or collections of stripped-down Beethoven and Mozart. It was supposed to be good for us, and it was better music than a lot of other options, but it was meaningless to a boy who had never heard a note of classical music. I did better with cowboy songs and patriotic music; at least I knew what those were supposed to sound like. Find what you're supposed to sound like and play with the sound of you, cutting loose.

Be careful, though. Such freewheeling, unfettered expression has a way of being released in the world. Or don't be careful. Maybe the writing you do just for yourself is meant to find entirely new audiences. Either way, your choice.

Interlude

The Writer's Seven (or However Many) Deadly Sins

IF YOU HANG AROUND the writing racket long enough, you will see every sort of writing success and failure imaginable—and some you can't imagine. I spent forty years teaching courses in writing and in literature where writing was a major component. Both during and after that time, I have been writing more or less steadily, sometimes frantically, once in a while ecstatically. Through all that time, I have seen—and accomplished—all manner of failure. For some reason, students would sometimes come to my office to apologize for their poor (in their estimation) efforts, as if they had let me down personally. Often it turned out that the writing was anything but a failure, but it didn't strike the student as a winner. Lacking any means of absolving themselves, they were asking me to do so for them. After offering what help I could, I obliged. In one terrible case, a brilliant mature student, although far too young for this fate, closed my door (something I never did on my own) and told me that trying to read and write for my course had revealed a change in her brain, an early-onset, not-yet-specified dementia. We wept together. Usually, such talks were much more mundane, with students seeking help after tying themselves up in knots. Help was one thing I had plenty of, both on my own and in sending them to our excellent writing center where their peers had knowledge and skills under less threatening rubrics than "professor."

But here's the thing about those visits: they rarely involved technical issues of committing prose to paper. Their knots were more existential than procedural. Mostly, they had thought themselves into corners and couldn't turn around and walk out. When we would get down to the specific issues they were having, they came down to one or two of the same handful of stumbling blocks I heard confessed again and again. Although never quite sure of the number, I came to think of them as the Seven Deadly Sins of writing. You may find them dispiritingly familiar. But take heart—they could have been the Dirty Dozen.

1. **Worry**
2. **Self-doubt**
3. **Overconfidence**
4. **Muddiness**
5. **Vagueness**
6. **Poor structure**
7. **Dishonesty**

Notice that nowhere on this list is there a mention of semi-colons. Or subject-verb agreement. Or sentence fragments. All of those things can be fixed. What *kills* writing is more basic than those surface-level errors, even if those tend to be the first thing people notice. But they only exist once the piece of writing does. The Deadly Seven prevent writing from occurring in the first place. Or, like overconfidence and dishonesty, they create something that is rotten at its heart, and no amount of surface grace can improve that sort of decadence.

Self-doubt is the companion that never leaves, that tries to insinuate its way into every moment of the writing process. Think of it as the infestation of termites trying to chew down your house of words. It is also, however—and this is why it is so insidious—related to a necessary caution that writers need: Is this the right word? Am I conveying what I intend to? Is there a better paragraph arrangement here? And so on. As with anything taken to extremes, caution can become disabling. The mind is a delicate instrument and responds badly to excesses of any kind.

Overconfidence often follows self-doubt as the writer begins to feel more in control of the process, more assured about their abilities. The result can be a pendulum swing to excessive, unwarranted assuredness. Then, when doubt begins to sink in, they crumble. Either that or their overconfidence leads the writer to attempt too much, in too small a space with too few tools. My most notorious failure: the inability to write a book on contemporary Irish poetry that I *knew* I could write. That disaster led to my titles that begin, "How to Read" and end, "Like a Professor." I assumed that I had an idea structure that, in the end, never materialized. The solution to both self-doubt and overconfidence, two sides of the same counterfeit quarter, is a dispassionate inventory of the writer's skills and acumen. If we can identify the strength of the base from which we write, we can avoid under- or overestimating our ability to do the job.

Muddiness results from lack of clear thinking, which can take a thousand forms: poor logic, unclear explanations, ambiguous motives, failures to wrestle the material into shape. As with numerous other sins here, no amount of surface repair can correct a structural problem. The corrective action is a simple, unpleasant question: Do I understand what I am saying well enough to convey it to my readers? Too often, the answer is negative. The tricky part of muddiness is that, if our thinking is muddled, we may not see clearly enough to fix it. Most times, however, dismantling the writing back down to the level of naked ideas—that is, unadorned by rhetoric that can obscure weaknesses—will reveal where the writer has gone awry. You can also address muddiness by purely formal strategies. For instance, rewrite the paper or whatever it is as a series of short, simple, declarative sentences, minus transitions. Stated so baldly, there is no place for mud to hide. You will find it and can address it. Then you can build it up into something that sounds as if written by a grown-up and not a fourth grader. First, though, back to fourth grade, which wasn't so bad after all.

Vagueness can take a number of forms, but they often stem from preferring generalities to specifics, which results in the lack of detail. That term may suggest insufficient use of evidence, and that is one manifestation, but there can be others. We may fail to spell out our logic step-by-step, the way we wanted in geometry class to skip from step one of a proof to step twelve because it all seemed self-evident to us. Maybe that wasn't you, but it was most certainly me. Or vagueness can manifest as a shortage of content words. The solution is usually to burrow into the text, into the meat and potatoes of the subject, into the specifics of the issue, pushing closer when our first impulse was to work at a distance.

Poor structure dooms many writing projects from the beginning. The writer has not found the mechanism for ordering the ideas. This issue presents more commonly in analytical or argumentative writing than in narratives. Absent or faulty structure undermines the writer's aspirations for the piece.

I once or twice read for a "writing contest" in the local schools. I put that term in quotation marks because, while winners really were announced, some teachers compelled their students to enter, which obviates the notion of a contest somewhat. Besides, every entrant got an award (where writing is involved, I think participation patches, those sources of irritation for persons of a certain age, are perfect). If they wrote, if they expressed themselves, and especially if they enjoyed doing so, good on 'em, I say. One memorable year, I read entries by third graders, among whom, alas, structural thinking is not a common virtue. This did not slow them down one bit, but it hindered their poor reader a good deal. That was okay, though, and no fault of the students who, at that age, in many cases have not reached the developmental stage where they can inevitably sequence and structure ideas or experience. Some have, and all will sooner or later, but not right then.

You are not in third grade, having long since passed that developmental stage that I needed my grade-three writers to have reached. Even so, not every first attempt at structure works out. The best advice I have is to abstract out every key point in a work, keeping the list in order—a sort of outline-after-the-fact. In that form, any organizational wobbles should become clearer and therefore remediable. Coming up with poor structure in the first place isn't a sin; sticking with it once it proves unwieldy or unclear or simply unsuitable is. All the fine writing in the world can't make structural weakness into strength. That's like adding lots of fancy details to a house with a crumbling foundation: eventually, the whole thing will tumble down around your ears.

Dishonesty in writing is the one unforgivable sin. If we intend to deceive our readers, the writing has no legitimacy. If we hide the truth from ourselves in order to cut corners, we allow our own folly to mislead others. Either way, there is no remedy available except to begin again with better intentions. Writers live within a basic compact with readers, and dishonest behavior breaks faith with them. Alas, we are awash in dishonest communications these days, which some commentators have dubbed "the misinformation age." It is worse than that, actually a "disinformation age," meaning that the spread of misinformation is intentional and aimed at doing harm. Neither our governing institutions nor our civil society can survive for long under such an assault on truth. Every part of an editorial or report can be perfectly written, but if the thing is corrupt at its very center, it can come to no good. All the more reason for those of us of goodwill and moral intent to cling to honesty as tightly as we can.

You will notice that this elaboration is only six, not seven, items long. If you're really paying attention, you will notice that the skipped sin is **Worry**, the first on the list. What gives? Worry is in a sense outside the writing process, too often stopping it before it can begin. We worry about a host of potential negatives when we write. Will my teacher like it? What sort of grade will it get? Will I get likes on social media? Can I really do this? Do I have the right to do this? Have I really figured this out? Do I need to give it more time? Why do I feel so inadequate? These are the questions posed by Gail Godwin's Watcher at the Gate, the voice of doubt and worry and anxiety trying to prevent writers from writing. That's why worry was first on the list: if it wins, all the others are moot. **You cannot let worry win.** There are no easy formulas for achieving that. Sometimes, you just have to power through and start writing even though you have no confidence. Push worry aside with extreme prejudice. Or a bulldozer. I find that swearing helps, but that may just be me. Just start. Push one word onto screen or paper, then another and another. It often gets easier as the words pile up. If not, keep slogging forward. The best way to defeat worry long-term is to finish a project and then another and another. To do that, you have to start, however formidable the task seems. You know you can. You've done it before. And you're about to do it again.

WHAT TO WRITE
AND HOW

6

Tell Yourself What You Want to Say

I write to discover what I know.
—FLANNERY O'CONNOR

THE MOST IMPORTANT ELEMENT in any piece of communication is having something to say. The second is knowing what that something is. There are many techniques for discovering that golden nugget, probably as many as there are nugget seekers. One of my dissertation advisors told me to write the thesis statement for the dissertation on the chalkboard in my office, and then every day when I came to the office, revise it until it was perfect. I shared my office with two other grad students and shyness prevented that approach, but I found a way. For every project, every one of us needs to find a way to that certain knowledge. You can't inform, sway, elevate, or devastate your readers unless you understand your own aims.

Let us say at the outset that not every writing task is dependent on the writer's vision. If this is your month to take the department meeting minutes, the only idea you need is: I have to write this out before I forget key details. There is definitely an art to producing readable and, to the extent possible, entertaining minutes, but the primary goal is accuracy: Who said what and in what context, what actions were voted on and what were the outcomes of those votes? Similarly, an obituary for a family member does not need a strong thesis. Again, accuracy is the goal, along with providing a brief narrative of a life. And surviving the ordeal of writing it. On the other hand, writing a eulogy requires more organization of thought and a clearer sense of a narrative thread. Most people will find it helps to spend a little time finding the through line of their summation of the loved one's life. That distinction brings us to a key point: **the nature of the task dictates how information is managed**.

A similar dichotomy to the obituary/eulogy pairing would be a scientific lab report versus a scientific paper or an account of a scientific discovery for a popular audience. Lab reports are cookbook writing, and for good reason. The purpose of the task is to convey the factual details of an experiment. To that end, the report is divided into predictable sections, such as Title, Introduction, Procedure (or Methods and Materials), Results, Discussions/Analysis, Conclusions, and Graphs and Charts, each presented with as much verbal economy as one can manage without cutting valuable details. This is not the place for involved introductory strategies or complex sentences or description-heavy writing (what the science types always complain to the writing staff as being "flowery writing"). This is meat-and-potatoes, subject-verb-object writing. Here is the hypothesis to be confirmed or rejected, step-by-step. The names used for those stages and their order may vary slightly from instructor to instructor, but the basic pattern is rigid enough that many instructors or departments have a template for lab students to follow. You won't get that for an analytical essay on *Middlemarch*.

Other forms of science writing will have different expectations. A scientific paper (an essay based on research and aimed at fellow professionals) typically involves constructing an argument that the research findings prove or refute some hypothesis. While there is a common basis between the lab report and the paper, the latter is more involved as well as intended not merely to inform but to persuade readers. The one formula everyone likely knows, $E = mc^2$, first appeared in 1905 in such a paper, "Does the Inertia of a Body Depend upon its Energy Content?," in the journal *Annalen der Physik* (*Annals of Physics*). In it, Einstein argued for that specific formula as explaining the mass-energy relationship, which had been a topic of discussion among many members of the field. So far, the math seems to be holding up okay.

An article or talk or book aimed at explaining important scientific concepts or discoveries to nonscientists would require a different approach to conveying information. And since nearly everything in contemporary science is beyond the understanding of the rest of us, this has been a growth industry, particularly in that strangest of sciences, physics of the grandest and tiniest systems. Michio Kaku, professor of theoretical physics at the City College of New York, has written works such as *Physics of the Future* (2011) that attempt to unravel the mysteries of subatomic physics, including such rarified topics as string theory, for readers whose mathematical attainment goes no further than Algebra II, if that. Neil deGrasse Tyson, director of the Hayden Planetarium, has worked at the other end of the size continuum, working to make such mind-bending phenomena as the Big Bang and black holes comprehensible to scientific civilians in books like *Death by*

Black Hole (2007) and *Astrophysics for People in a Hurry* (2017). Works like these are vastly different from scientific papers for fellow experts so the communication strategies will also diverge. But strategies there must be, and writers of either will have to be clear in their own minds as to the goals and arguments exercised in either sort of writing.

While there are writing projects where careful planning as to the arguments or strategies will be a minor factor, for most public writing, we—any of us, no matter how clever—will have to work to hone our message, to present the cleanest, most succinct formulation of our main idea and every subsidiary idea that grows out of it. The longer the work will be, the more desperately that clarity is needed. We say that we are doing all this for readers, and to a point that is true, but mostly we do it to save ourselves from falling into a narrative or argumentative or expositional slough of despond. No one wants to be a swamp creature.

That makes sense, I guess, but how do we avoid bogging down?

By building a set of wings. The way to not bog down in all the details and moment-to-moment considerations is to rise above all that and maintain a bird's-eye view with part of your brain while the bulk of it is pursuing those right-here, right-now problems. If you construct a sufficiently dynamic, compelling master statement, that thing we usually call a *thesis statement*, you can keep track of how *this* paragraph, *this* argument is tying in with the overarching idea structure. In fact, if that master statement is good enough, you shouldn't have to keep track, because some subconscious part of your brain will be tracking it for you.

Etymologically, "thesis" derives unchanged but for spelling from the Greek, where it meant "a thing put forth or placed," as in for discussion. It has come to mean, in this context, "an assertion or theory put forward as a proposition to be proved." In practical terms it is the idea that drives all the other ideas in a work, the *one ring to rule them all*. Now, this being English, it has other meanings, the most vexatious of which is "lengthy scholarly work," similar to or exactly like "dissertation." That one is from Latin, ours from Greek. Just be thankful that the Angles and Saxons who invaded Britain had no idea regarding graduate study or things would really be messy. But we need only trouble ourselves with one meaning, which is "controlling idea in a work of nonfiction," the thing that assists writers in organizing and managing their thoughts, that allows them to look down at their work and determine whether or not it is sticking to the point. Which brings us to a question:

What Makes a Good Thesis?

LET'S GO BACK TO THAT advice on my dissertation's thesis statement (here's where we get into the thesis/thesis overlapping confusion). Why was that advice so critical? It has to do with the nature of dissertations. Or possibly the nature of one specific dissertator. "Dissertation" is just a fancy way of saying "book that no one wants to read or is likely to publish." They do get published as books sometimes (mine was, eventually), but they generally require a good deal of revision and rewriting and especially of cutting markers that identify the work as a glorified student paper. Like books, they are nearly always written in chapters and then pulled together around a common argumentative thread. That already inclines the chapters to be less than cohesive, a tendency that is magnified if those chapters were written for different occasions and even published as stand-alone articles, as several of mine were. The more diffuse the separate parts are, the stronger that thread needs to be tying them together. In my case, the thread needed to be more like a ship's hawser.

What should a thesis contain? Instead of naming three parts, as many sources will do, and which we will get to, let us focus on qualities. A solid thesis should be:

- Confident. You are staking a claim, not asking for a hall pass.
- Single-minded. It has one job to do and must do it perfectly.
- Dynamic. Its verb should suggest *action* as well as pushing readers to the next paragraph, the next page, the next chapter.
- Flawless. A careless error at this stage can scuttle the whole project.
- Economical. That is, it must reach its goals with as little verbiage as possible to achieve its task.

These qualities are not mysterious. Confidence is critical: Why should a reader believe you if you don't seem to believe yourself? Typically, a thesis is a single sentence, perhaps a couple in a longer work. There's no room to introduce anything except the main point. Dynamic? The thesis stands as the hinge point of your piece, the culmination of everything that has been said before and the promise of everything that will be said. Beyond that crucial function, it must make the idea be dynamic in itself. The easiest way to accomplish that task is to introduce causality either with the factors that have caused the current situation or those that the situation will cause. There are, of course, others. Teacher types like theses that post the three items students will discuss in their essays, or maybe I should say that teachers adhere to that model because standardized tests seem to require it. But what if you are writing something longer and you have not three supporting items but twelve or twenty? That thesis would become a trifle unwieldy, no?

Having looked at the qualities, let's consider the practical aspects of your thesis, that most practical of statements.

- Location. There is no hard-and-fast rule that a main statement of purpose must land at the end of the first paragraph (or chapter, if in a book), no matter who may have told you there is. But on average, that is where most theses reside. Readers have largely come to expect it to be there through experience. The rest of the opening paragraph has been building to this moment, so it makes sense to stake your big claim there. This is the end of the beginning and the beginning of everything else.

- Closed-form or open-ended? Put otherwise, statement or question? There are two major types of essay, deductive and inductive. In the former, the writer makes an assertion about the topic and then sets about to prove it. In the latter, the writer poses a question to be answered and then spends the rest of the essay arriving at the answer. In this form, the "thesis" is actually a promissory note, an IOU for a thesis arriving in the conclusion. There is no "correct" form here, only different approaches and different rewards. And perils. If the writers are genuinely searching for answers, as opposed to assuming a pose, then the inductive form makes total sense. That is rarely the case. More often, they wish to ease potentially hostile readers into arriving at a position where they may not have intended to go. The most obvious hazard with an inductive essay is that it can seem contrived; the central idea has been baked in all along and the writer has merely been hiding this fact. A less obvious danger is that habits formed in years of writing deductive essays lead the writer to never quite get around to that thesis, because (habit says) it's back up there in the opening, except it isn't. On the other side, the great hazard of the deductive form is that it can sound like every other essay in the world. You pays your money and you takes your chances. If there were an assured path to success, we would all follow it.

Last chance for change. The decision about the form and content of the thesis locks in the shape of the essay or article. The writer can't, for instance, set out a theory to be proved and then get a couple of pages in and decide, "this should be an inductive essay instead." Or rather, she can, but that entails going back at least to the thesis and changing the form to accommodate that new approach.

Center the idea. Lose yourself. The best advice I can offer a developing writer is to never appear in a thesis statement. Make the subject of the essay the subject of the thesis, and make sure there is a real verb. When I was teaching comparatively inexperienced writers in literature classes, there was one construction that made my heart sink: "In this paper, I will discuss . . ." At that point, I knew this was a doomed enterprise, if only because I had already told them not to do it, but mostly because the paper would never really make a convincing point. And I was right about ninety-nine percent of the time. About one paper in a hundred, though, would use that form to show that something valuable could come from such unpromising handling. That paper was nearly always written by someone who didn't need to be in an introductory literature class and had already written dozens of successful essays about novels and poems. What that student was doing was telling me what you and I already know: **you can break any writing rule if you're good enough**. Smart aleck.

Consider this last example a bit more. Not the one-percenters, but the bulk of those who fell into the "I will discuss" trap. First of all, let me add that such a phrase can be used earlier in the opening. I don't like it because it is uneconomical; that is, it rarely appears in a sentence that actually moves the argument or narrative forward. But as the second sentence in an opening, it is not the deal-breaker it would be in a thesis.

As the thesis, however, that gambit violates two critical principles. First, it results in a noun clause with no verb and therefore no idea. Not even an idea of whether the paper *has* an idea: "In this paper, I will discuss Fitzgerald's use of metaphor in *The Great Gatsby*." There is no verb here, as there almost never is in such theses. The appeal, it seems to me, for the writer is that he isn't pinned down by anything too specific. Where he sees comfort or safety, though, I see a cry for help, a plea that says: I hope I find out what this paper is about before I get to the end. So do we. Second, the noun clause just sits there, inert, when the paper most needs to be dynamic. We should be launching forward into the meat of the argument or biography or history, and instead we're stuck in one place like the house by the side of the road. Instead of that lame construction, consider this option: "Fitzgerald employs metaphor in *The Great Gatsby* to avoid having to demonstrate that Nick Carraway, our otherwise eloquent narrator, is incapable of articulating matters of heart, spirit, and desire." Whether you agree with the assertion or not is immaterial. What matters is that it *does* assert something and shows every evidence that it intends to support it vigorously. In the earlier version, we can't be sure the writer has anything to support, much less a plan to do so.

Signaling intent, in turn, pushes the essay forward into its next phase and shows readers the path forward. Perhaps more to the point, it signals to the writer where he is to go and what he has to do. That is the sort of dynamism that any piece of writing needs.

What if I'm not writing an argument? It's just a biographical sketch of an old rodeo rider.

So, what, rodeo riders don't deserve the respect of an idea? That's cold. But think of my Fitzgerald example. The writer is exploring the use of metaphor in *Gatsby*. That does not make the effort, however, a mere report. Instead, he introduces a real, live idea about how metaphor functions in the novel. In the case of your rodeo profile, you are going to want your main point to tell us why this old rider is worth knowing, why your profile is worth reading: "Through a career that includes twenty-two broken bones, countless concussions, a ruptured spleen, and thousands of nights spent in cheap hotels, Red Fowler has achieved a sort of zen state about a way of life that suggests anything but stillness." That may not describe your rodeo performer, but you would want something like that, something that makes us want to know him better.

Cast your mind back to the middle grades, sixth through eighth. Your teachers were beginning to shift (or try to) away from your "writing" merely being a recap of what you read to some original statement—by and from you—about what you read. You maybe didn't notice because the shift was incremental. Baby steps. In high school, you were encouraged to think for yourself, to have something to say. It needed to engage with the material and, although perhaps you didn't quite pick this up (nor did I), be something that in the whole world, only you would say quite the way you did. If you look at serious writing, the sort that appears in national magazines from *The New Yorker* and *The Atlantic* to *Better Homes and Gardens* and *Field & Stream*, every piece with a byline bears the imprint of its writer. Why? Because this is what grown-ups do. They have a point of view on the material they turn into articles. It is possible to write a news story of a few paragraphs on, say, a car crash and make it sound completely objective and impersonal. The longer the article, however, the harder that stance is to maintain. Pick up a copy of *The New Yorker* (available at newsstands, bookstores, and public libraries, which have the advantage of being free) and read the first four or five paragraphs of each article. What you'll find is that, contrary to what we all thought we learned about journalism, every review, every major article, every profile is suffused with the viewpoint and personality of its writer. We read not merely to discover facts but to see how someone, a person who has researched and thought and lived with the material for a period of weeks or months, understands those facts in context.

Every piece of writing is an argument, even if its only point is, "I'm worth reading."

A great thesis, and therefore a great essay, history, narrative, review, or profile, brings an informed intelligence into contact with significant material. That's what you want from your main idea, your thesis: the chance for greatness. It is a rare piece of nonfiction that can rise higher than its thesis, its main point. More often, writing falls short of that potential. For that reason alone, you owe it to yourself to write the strongest thesis you can. After all, what advantage is there in doing less?

7

Voice Actor

*No one will ever write in just the way that you do, or
in just the way that anyone else does. . . . Writing is a
matter strictly of developing oneself. You compete only
with yourself. You develop yourself by writing.*
—JOHN MCPHEE

ONE OF THE THINGS that makes us special is our voice. It makes
us sound like us. We can tell, often after the first syllable, which
of our numerous friends and relatives and professional associates
is on the phone even if we didn't see a name or number on the
screen. Voice is a combination of genetics, socialization, and personal decision-making. In other words, we're born with a certain
voice, which is shaped by the voices around us from infancy onward, but we can make alterations, within limits, to how high or
low it is, whether it centers in the chest or the nasal cavity, and so
on. Well, guess what: we have a writing voice, too. And like our
speaking voice, it makes our writing sound like us. It expresses
who we are, how we think those thoughts that we do, how we

employ *these* words in *this* order and not some others in some other order. It's indispensable, really. Then why is so much writing denatured, devoid of personality, generic-sounding? It's easy to find out what you "sound" like and how to use that sound. It only took me thirty years or so.

Voice is what John McPhee is really talking about in the quote that begins this chapter, the set of properties that is unlike that of any other writer. We *are* distinctive, individual, unique, if only we choose to grasp the opportunity to be so. We don't have to sound like the back of a cereal box or like every university regulation ever written. We don't have to sound generic and shouldn't, because we are *not* generic. We each are the only one of us there ever has been or ever will be, even if we are an identical twin or the original of a clone. Or vice versa. Those others, however close to us, do not have exactly our experience because we know ourselves from the inside and our twin only from the outside, which is the opposite of their experience. McPhee, one of our greatest writers and teachers of nonfiction, exhorts us as he has exhorted his writing students for nearly fifty years to grasp what makes us unique and build our writing personality on that foundation. Given that many of the alumni of his course at Princeton have gone on to become world-famous writers and editors, we might want to heed his advice.

Voice is an outgrowth of our speaking voice, but it is not identical to it. Writing is not merely speech transcribed, even when it presents the illusion that it is. Maybe especially then. Writers work incredibly hard to sound as if they're not working at all. New writers often mistake the pretense for the actuality, with results ranging from the laughable to the catastrophic. Some writers work for years to find their signature style, their voice. Some get there quicker by means of a deep dive, which is another way of saying that they compress years of work into months or even weeks in a headlong rush to establish their characteristic sound. A few are seemingly born with it, but not many. Even Ernest Hemingway didn't sound like Hemingway until he did. My colleague and friend Frederic J. Svoboda wrote his first book, *Hemingway and* The Sun Also Rises*: The Crafting of a Style*, on how Hemingway forged his distinctive style as he labored to find the best way of telling his great novel.

A great many elements go into the creation of a writing voice. The one constant is words; lacking intonation of speech, writing is entirely a matter of words on the page. Words on the page, however, are among the wonders of the world. *Diction* (the specific words chosen), *syntax* (the order of those words), *rhythm*, and *auditory properties* (alliteration, rhyme, consonance, assonance, even meter) are all key elements in a writer's voice, which all comes down to the words one uses and how one deploys them. Voice is the means by which a writer makes herself known to the world, so she does well to take some care in its crafting.

It may seem as if we are born with a voice, as we are born with a speaking voice, in which case maybe we are stuck with this accident of birth, but that's not true. We can alter our writing voice. In fact, alteration is all but inevitable. The same is true of speaking voices. I grew up outside Dayton, Ohio, went to school in northern New England with friends hailing from everywhere between Cape Cod and Arkansas and San Francisco as well as between Ontario and Alberta, then spent my entire postcollege life in Michigan's Lower Peninsula. My speech is not what it would have been had I remained in southwest Ohio all those years. So, too, has my writing voice changed, not only because of those geographic influences but from all my reading, the famous writers and the not-so-famous friends whose styles have imposed themselves on my mind. The only constant, as the ancient Greek philosopher Heraclitus may or may not have said (he gets blamed for a lot of things), is change. If change is inevitable, we should be able to manage it, and we can. As we grow and learn and develop and even decline, our presentation of our selves will alter; that alteration will present itself in our written voice. Heraclitus also said, so we are told, that one cannot step into the same river twice. Both the river and the one stepping in will have changed. Know it. Embrace it. Act upon it.

Most of us have several writing personas. I could use "personae," but then I would have a different persona from the one I choose to employ here. How we present ourselves in a formal, academic paper will be different from how we present ourselves when we write to friends or post on social media. In ordinary conversation, we show different aspects to our rowdy pals and to Great-Aunt Mildred. Does the difference mean that one is true and another false? Not really. What we are doing is selecting which parts of ourselves to reveal in different contexts. The basic fact, however, is that they must all be true, that is, partake to some degree in our real selves. If they don't, someone will spot us as a fake. We won't sound right. Same thing with writing. Our persona in any given context must still be us, with certain elements pushed forward or dropped further into the background.

Your writing persona must be someone you are comfortable inhabiting. That is, they can't be too different from your basic personality.

Why can't I just be me?

You can. In fact, "me" is the best thing you can be, but which "me"? There are versions and versions of any of us, and the parts that emerge in any context depend to a large extent on that context. That doesn't mean that they are false or that some are truer than others, so long as they are all part of the master persona, the one of which all the others partake. Thus also will it be with voice: it will vary in different contexts, but it has to grow out of who you are and what you know.

Some writers have completely recognizable voices, and readers notice quickly. In the same way that one doesn't have to be a musical scholar to tell that Willie Nelson and Johnny Cash don't sound alike. Or Johnny Mathis. Or Joni Mitchell. No special equipment required. Same with reading; the only talent required is attention. How do we know, for instance, that a passage we're reading is Hemingway? Sure, the name on the cover helps, but our inner ear does the work. Some might think of it as a voice in our heads that renders print into sound, but I prefer it as an auditory instrument. We notice with Hemingway the short sentences, the simple vocabulary, the lack of adornment (modifiers like adjectives, adverbs, and subordinate clauses). Sentences are brief and declarative, but the specific words he uses also matter. In the last paragraph of *A Farewell to Arms*, the hero, Frederic Henry, has just lost his lover and her stillborn baby, and after chasing the two nurses attending to the body out of the hospital room, he has a few moments alone with the deceased Catherine:

> But after I had got them out and shut the door and turned off the light it wasn't any good. It was like saying good-bye to a statue. After a while I went out and left the hospital and walked back to the hotel in the rain.

This is one of the most devastating endings in literature not despite the flatness of the writing but because of it. The words are of the most ordinary sort; only one, "statue," is the least bit remarkable, in part because, without telling us so, the word conjures up another lifeless human form, which is what his beloved has become, no longer a person but a thing to be dealt with by strangers. Otherwise, the narrative is carried by the verbs—"got," "shut," "turned," "was," "went," "left," and "walked"—which could not be more common or less picturesque. Not "strolled" or "trudged" or "stumbled," but "walked." The narrator, Henry, is so numbed that no other words will come, and this is no time for the evocative. In fact, what Hemingway seeks to evoke is a sense of nothingness.

Admittedly, this is a passage of fiction, but it works for nonfiction as well. Here is part of the title essay of Joan Didion's *The White Album*. She is writing about an ostensible recording session by The Doors, delayed at the point of this passage by the very late arrival of lead singer Jim Morrison:

> Morrison sat down again on the leather couch and leaned back. He lit a match. He studied the flame awhile and then very slowly, very deliberately lowered it to the fly of his black vinyl pants. [Keyboardist Ray] Manzarek watched him. The girl who was rubbing Manzarek's shoulders did not look at anyone. There was a sense that no one was going to leave the room, ever. It would be some weeks before The Doors finished recording this album. I did not see it through.

Didion is less stingy with modifiers than Hemingway, but she shares his affinity for short, declarative sentences that mean more than they say. A lesser writer might have said, by way of a final sentence, that she was unwilling to just hang around while these self-absorbed young people finally got around to doing something. Instead, she simply says, "I did not see it through." The effect is much more brutal in its simplicity and understatement.

Chances are that you are not a Hemingway or a Didion. On the other hand, you are probably not Hunter S. Thompson, with his wild flights of rhetoric, nor Tom Wolfe, the chameleon mimicking the speech of his subjects as his style. The truth is that most of the writing styles and voices that we remember are extravagant, by which I mean neither praise nor condemnation, while most of ours are not. Which is fine. Stylistic extravagance can be highly rewarding, if one is sufficiently talented and lucky enough to capture the mood of the reading public at a given moment, but it is always high-risk. Failure in this instance sounds like bad imitation or simple gibberish. Jack Kerouac was unquestionably a genius, but his is the voice that crashed a thousand ships. Even so, it behooves every writer to discover his or her native voice and to decide what, if anything, might be done to alter it as circumstance or desire dictates.

Finding Your Voice

ALL RIGHT, THEN, WHAT IS your voice? What, you don't know? Of course you don't. Almost no one does, until they need one or have it pointed out to them that they already have a sound. At that point, they—and here I mean "we," because this describes me at a much earlier point in life—need to set about discovering what their sound is and what tools are needed for that discovery. And most of us find that we've not a clue how to begin.

Nor are writing books terribly helpful. William Zinsser addresses it late in *On Writing Well*, but chiefly as injunctions to write the best prose one can manage and to avoid certain mannerisms—clichés and condescension—that we can mostly figure out on our own. Anne Lamott is at least as vague in *Bird by Bird*, but her book is taken from her fiction-writing courses, and voice in fiction is a story-by-story decision and not a more fixed identity as with nonfiction writers. In his excellent *Draft No. 4: On the Writing Process*, John McPhee skips the matter entirely, diving into the weightier matters of conducting interviews and finding the right structures. Since his book is quite brief, the omission is understandable if still odd, given that he has a voice and style that fits him, as someone said of the Elizabethans, like a tailored garment. Some composition texts from the seventies and eighties went into more detail, and some didn't, depending on the predilection of the author. In other words, we're on our own.

Fear not, the process is manageable. First of all, don't worry about your voice until you've had a chance to write enough to have something to analyze. For most people, unless they are very young, they already have enough material to work with. The volume of letters, course papers, online screeds, and so on that one generates can be a little overwhelming. Once you have enough writing time that you have choices of work to analyze, pick out one or more. If your writing is very consistent stylistically, one might be all you need. If you are still developing, you may want more samples so that you can examine the direction you seem to be heading rather than simply picking one moment in time. Pick items that are fairly clean editorially so that you are not spending all your time stopping to ask, "Why on earth did I write *that*?" Then having chosen the material, follow a process that will get you the answers that you seek. Here is a list I think works, but you may think of different steps. By the way, it is the same process for figuring out how other writers achieve their effects.

- Read. In this case, I mean read aloud. This is best undertaken without witnesses, because I can guarantee that it will involve some measure of embarrassment or discomfort, neither of which is lessened by an audience. As you read, you will probably stumble over stylistic infelicities, those little accidents and errors that are unintended. Ignore them. Read for the sounds, the rhythms, the music of the words. At every stopping point, if not during the reading, ask yourself these questions: Is that what I sound like? Is that what I want to sound like?

- Deconstruct. Having heard the passage, take it apart brick by brick. What words do you use? Short or long? What about the order you use them in? Are your sentences simple or compound or complex? Are they mixed or all of one type? Are your verbs active? Are your verbs active enough? Are enough of your verbs active? Are your nouns concrete or abstract? Is that lump a piece of stone or a chunk of granite? What tone do you adopt? Formal or informal? Serious or comic or mixed?

- Identify items to keep or discard. Having identified a foundational sound of your writing voice, and then having taken apart the passage that showed you that sound, decide what stays and what goes. The criterion is simple: Does this individual piece help establish my voice or would some other word or phrase or sentence work better? If the latter, make the replacement.

- Reassemble. Having sorted the rhetorical wheat from the chaff, put the pieces back together—the best pieces in the best order.
- Wait. One day at a minimum, but three would be better. Let the text marinate and your mind clear (mostly the latter).
- Repeat. You now believe that the new version is superior to the original. Put it to the text test: read this one aloud just as before. If there is *anything* about that reading that you don't like, go through the remaining steps again. If you're in love with it, move on to another piece, preferably another type of writing so that you see whether this new voice can be adapted to various tasks. A one-trick writing pony isn't terribly useful.

Once you are satisfied that you have found a workable identity, it will be time to test out this new you. You need to write something from scratch using this new voice. Can you make it work? Can you control it, or do you fall back into old habits? Does it achieve what you want it to? There is no way to know these answers until you have stress-tested it. Repeatedly. A writing voice isn't a one-time decision; it's a habit of mind, a learned and practiced behavior. You will stumble and fall sometimes, go too far in one direction or another and have to reel yourself back in, perform brilliantly only to stumble again.

You should never find yourself a slave to your voice. Even after rocker Vince Furnier had legally changed his name to Alice Cooper, he had to break up with "Alice Cooper," his stage persona, because its excesses threatened to destroy his life. It is one thing to create a persona, quite another to lose your true self in

it. Chances are that your writing persona and voice are less compelling, and far less destructive, than "Alice Cooper" proved to
be. If you understand that it is *your* creation, you own it and can
do with it—modify, enhance, simplify, or reject entirely—as you
will. Never meant to be static and permanent, it will grow as your
writing history does.

John McPhee began this chapter by reminding us that we
are, each one, singular, a one-time-only offer to everyone else. We
know this, even if we lack confidence to fully embrace it. But embrace it we must, if we are going to make good on that possibility
of bringing something unique in all of human history. After all,
who are we to deny that gift to the world?

8

Beginning Before You Begin

Beginning a novel is always hard. It feels like going nowhere. I always have to write at least 100 pages that go into the trashcan before it finally begins to work. It's discouraging, but necessary to write those pages. I try to consider them pages −100 to 0 of the novel.

—BARBARA KINGSOLVER

KIDS TODAY, ALWAYS IN such a hurry! And fifty years ago, when I was one. And so on. But not just kids. Everyone has always been in a mad dash to finish whatever writing needs to be done. Get the assignment, sit down, and pound out . . . something. Because something, anything is what we are willing to live with. That doesn't mean it's good. Writing is not a single act but a sequence of them, a process, to use the term of art long preferred by writing instructors. This sequence does not begin nor end with composing a draft. It can't, if the final product is to possess any qualities that might make us proud.

The version of Creation as recorded in Genesis is the last

perfect first draft in the world. Even then, the final and crowning addition could have used some editing. Most of us nondeities, though, need to begin by admitting that our drafts are going to be lousy and can only become less so with work before and after their composing. In other words, we need a process.

What, exactly, is the writing process? Ask that question in a browser search, and you will get variants of the same answer: it is an examination of the too often unexamined steps by which an idea becomes a piece of finished writing. Among the assorted definitions, there are commonalities. One of those is that the process has steps. How many? Three or four or five, usually. Fewer and it isn't a process, more and it is too discouraging for words. Here's the version my search revealed most often: the writing process has three steps, called "prewriting," "drafting" (which in some cases is actually called "writing," because, you know, symmetry), and "post-writing." How's that for lame-naming? "Prewriting," the initial stage and therefore our first stop on the process tour, refers to everything that happens before and often alongside the drafting, which includes generating ideas, organizing thoughts on the topic, creating plans of attack and outlines—in short, everything in the initial creative process except writing the draft itself. It is a term that drives twenty-first-century composition specialists bonkers, and for good reason: it implies that whatever happens before drafting is not really writing. The entire process, they (and I with them) will argue, is writing. To my mind, the "pre-" and "post-" prefixes are largely nonsensical in addition to uninformative. So let's be a little more helpful in terms of terms. Let's call that first one **Invention**. This term has been around for a while, and I like it as describing the first stage of writing. It suggests moving from the slurry of vague ideas and dim motives and chaotic thinking toward a plan of action, while involving less hubris than, say, "Genesis."

Just for the record, the other three stages (clearly, I'm a four-leaf process guy) are **Drafting**, **Refining**, and **Polishing**. We'll get to them later, when such activities are appropriate. For now, there's starting to do.

What goes into invention? Besides computer solitaire, that is? Hey, don't rule it out *a priori*; many an insight has come while pulling a black jack down onto a red queen. Solitaire only requires about five percent of the ten percent of my brain that is ever in use at a given moment, so that leaves most of my limited intelligence to rattle around and possibly bump into an idea. Don't expect that stratagem to work with chess.

Nongaming methods encompass almost any technique you can imagine, a few you probably can't, and one or two that are nearly unthinkable.

Herewith, a partial taxonomy of the steps of invention. Don't feel bullied by the sheer volume; these are options to choose among, not goals that must be achieved.

- Activities can include **Daydreaming** (hard to document but always an option), **Brainstorming**, **Listing**, **Note Taking**, **Clustering**, **Freewriting**, **Looping**, **Journaling**, **Mapping and Diagramming**, **Outlining**, **Deep Drilling**, **Expanding**, and **Roaming and Rambling**.
- No one uses all of these prior to any given first draft. Reasons include time constraints and personal inclination. I, for instance, am allergic to anything that resembles drawing, so Mapping and Diagramming almost never happen in my process.

- **Brainstorming** is what it sounds like. Throw as much mental spaghetti as possible at your creative wall and see what, if anything, sticks. Form doesn't matter, nor do sentences nor phrasing nor spelling nor cusswords. Just sling it.

- **Listing** is brainstorming for the organized. Make lists of everything related to your topic, every single item you can think of before you begin. You'll think of more as you go, but this, like everything in this list, is just a device to get you started.

- **Note Taking** or even **Note Card Writing** is indispensable for gathering information, of course, but also very useful for arranging one's ideas and materials. John McPhee manages his note cards (not from other sources but simply from his front-line note taking) to discover his organizational scheme. He will come up with sometimes elaborate layouts for his note cards to represent the way his narratives will proceed. Anne Lamott uses note cards to record *anything* she wants to remember; they are less cumbersome than stenographer's notebooks and easy to slip into a pocket, even (as she tells it) while walking the dog. Her dog must be better behaved than mine generally are.

- **Clustering** is the process of gathering those rough lumps from the brainstorming or listing. You're taking separate items and trying to make them less separate. Think of it as sweeping debris into piles in order to turn them into something less random. Avoid clustering until you have generated enough bits and pieces; once you begin to impose order, that order itself may become the enemy of further creativity.

- **Freewriting** is like brainstorming but more like prose. If you are someone who is more comfortable when your writing looks like, well, writing, this may appeal to you. In essence, you conduct a timed-writing exercise on your topic, writing as much as you can as fast as you can for five or ten minutes. Structure doesn't matter, nor order nor politeness. What you wind up with is a chaotic word salad, from which you may glean bits and pieces for your draft.

- **Looping** is a sort of refinement of freewriting. Basically, you undertake a series of timed writings, each zeroing in on an aspect revealed in the previous one. In so doing, you cull unsuitable material and build up the good stuff. Looping mimics the process most of us follow consciously or not as we work our way into a draft. We keep chewing on an idea, working progressively from vague to specific, dreamy to workable. The added value is that the progress is demonstrable and recorded, so new developments don't slide away on the first distraction.

- **Journaling** is a way to keep a running conversation between writer and production. Essentially, one keeps a journal with entries, a writing-specific diary, to consult when drafting and revising. This is probably a technique best suited to long projects, but you may find other uses.

- **Mapping and Diagramming** are ways for visual thinkers to arrange their thoughts. Draw a map or diagram of where ideas and evidence lie in relation to one another. Then draw lines between the ones that show strong affinities. What lines you use (for instance, thin or thick to display strength of connection or merely lines of uniform thickness) will be your choice. As I mentioned before, I don't get it, but I have friends who swear by maps and/or diagrams. You may, too. Different strokes, you know.

- **Outlining**, the one you know (and may hate) from school, is a more or less formal process of placing ideas and examples in an orderly arrangement that can act as a roadmap for the first draft. What makes an outline more formal is if it is assigned by a teacher. If the writer is doing an outline for himself, however he expresses his order is fine; if a grade hangs in the balance, use all the letters and numerals in the prescribed manner. In my own work, I find that the longer the piece of writing, the more valuable all those capital and lowercase letters, Roman and Arabic numerals become.

- **Deep Drilling** is one of the ways to look for more in your invention work. If something excites you in the course of prepping for the draft, you can either go deep or wide. Here, you take the exciting bit and drill down to find what it contains and what has remained hidden until now. That can involve research or simply further thinking to answer the question: What more is there to know about this?

- **Expanding** is the wide option for finding more material. Think of your idea or plan as something that is folded up. Expanding unfolds it to lay out the whole operation by filling in the picture. Watch for connections to related topics and ideas. Sometimes those lead you off topic, but just as often they offer reasons to include material you had not originally thought of.

- **Roaming and Rambling.** There is a long history going back to the Greeks of peripatetic thinking, that is, musing while walking about. The poet William Wordsworth was famous for taking long walks in the Lake District in the west of England, after which he would sit down and write out poems. He said that the act of walking was the perfect medium for drumming out iambic verse (whose meter is an unstressed syllable followed by a stressed syllable: da-DUM), which has been the industry standard of English poetry for eight centuries. Ideas came to him as well, letting him write poems about, say, the ruins of Tintern Abbey and come up with lines like, "I wandered lonely as a cloud." Which is perfect iambic tetrameter (an iamb times four). One rule for R&R: **no headphones**. If you are piping sound into your ears, that's no longer Invention—it's avoiding the task at hand.

These techniques can be quite valuable. Why not just declare them successful and move on? Because success depends on the individual writer and situation. I am not a visual or spatial thinker, so mapping and diagramming won't work for me. That limitation has everything to do with me and not the techniques. At the same time, while I am often impatient with outlining, as I suggested above, there are times when it is the best way forward. Those results are situation-specific, since I am the same person in each case. Sometimes the situation that matters is not the writing assignment but the generative activity. I strongly recommend walking during various phases of the writing process, but conditionally. Yes, walking is healthier than just sitting there for twenty hours straight. On that basis, you can't go wrong. As a prewriting activity, on the other hand, it tends to be helpful only when undertaken alone. Okay, you can take your dog, but avoid human companionship. Why? Conversation is the enemy of thought. When I walk with the close-relative-by-marriage who is my daily companion, we talk about all sorts of things. Almost none of those things is my current writing, and even when it is, the results are unpromising. Please note, none of this is the fault of either party but merely a product of the human need to communicate. The dogs? They never talk, and my words to them are largely limited to monosyllables. Even with that caveat, walking might not work for you. No strategy is universally successful.

The techniques and strategies you adopt will, ultimately, come down to you. Which ones feel right for you? Which ones are dead ends? Most of all, which ones get you moving forward quickly? A lot of writing decisions are actually time decisions: What can I accomplish in the rapidly dwindling time before my assignment or report or letter has to be where it is going? And how can I best accomplish it? Keep in mind, though, that you will never know the real answers to those questions unless you try all of the methods. Meaning, really try them. Even if, like me, you don't think mapping is for you, go with it, just this once. Sometimes we surprise ourselves. This is what writing classes are good for, giving students the occasion—and even the requirement—to try different approaches that they might not try on their own. Comp instructors know that we all have our own learning styles, preferences, and phobias. Any approach to learning will work with part of the class and leave the rest cold. What teachers do, then, is to have everyone try everything, knowing that each student will discover preferences. What students learn, ultimately, by all this trial and error is not which techniques are superior but two more important things: first, that each individual will have favored approaches to invention, and second, that when a specific technique fails to yield results, there are others waiting to be tried.

If you're not in a course, no big deal. You can still try a lot of approaches to prepping for a draft. Don't worry if you're doing them right. Specifics matter a lot less than trying things that aren't all the same thing. Curvy lines or straight for maps and diagrams? Who cares? Only you, so you can't be wrong. Loop lines all around the paper or follow the shortest route: as long as you can also follow the logic behind your diagram, that's a good exercise.

Right there is the key fact about everything you do before the actual composing begins: **none of it is for anyone's eyes but yours**. Even if you have to turn in your prewriting to prove that you are actually experiencing the process, the only grading that happens is a checkmark in a gradebook. Oh, you might get some feedback if it's the one day a year that your composition instructor isn't overwhelmed by workload, but you still own it. The moment you put the first capital letter on your draft, you are writing for other people; until then, however, you rule!

Of the numerous techniques in that laundry list I offered up before, three more or less go together conceptually: looping, deep drilling, and expanding. We could throw in outlining, but it is slightly different. Your first steps, all that putting squiggles on paper and writing with the floodgates open and so on, are about generating basic material for your essay or letter or what have you. At some point, though, a writer has to move forward, toward something sharper, more focused, and more muscular.

Looping, the sequence of ever-more-focused freewriting exercises, moves steadily toward narrowing the topic down to its cleanest form. Freewriting by definition is messy; with the internal censors turned off, the mind will pull in peripheral and even extraneous material. Let it. Some of that will be garbage, but some may prove fruitful by adding to, substituting, or pruning the original scribblings. This approach may appeal to those who don't mind the extra work their hands undertake in exercise after exercise. It will drive others straight up the wall. For them, the tighter control of *deep drilling* may work better. In this instance, the writer selects portions of the freewriting to explore in depth and then, through targeted writing or research, discovers the avenues to develop the initial idea. Let's say your goal is an essay on reproductive surrogacy. In your freewriting, you briefly mentioned pros and cons for the surrogate mother. As you read through that portion of the exercise, you identify that by circling or underscoring or writing in the margin or using a fresh sheet of paper, and you jot down items to look into. One of those might be the question of how postpartum depression affects surrogates at different rates than women bearing their own babies. I have no idea, and my guess is that neither do you, so this would be an area to research before going forward—assuming it applies to the specific thesis that you pursue.

Expanding your first effort would head in the other direction, moving from some single point or narrow field to a wider discussion. Suppose that, in our example, you had already thought of postpartum depression, but you wanted, on reflection, to widen out to the mental health implications for all parties in the surrogacy arrangement. Do they exist for the parents? Are there other benefits or hazards for the surrogate? For that matter, how do children in such arrangements handle the knowledge of how they came into the world? These might come to nothing, or they could reveal intriguing paths of discovery. In any case, this approach resembles deep drilling in being more targeted than more free-writing with only a vague notion of focus. The writer would likely not expand the complete freewriting exercise, since it was pretty unfocused (if they are like any I ever came up with). Instead, what would be expanded would be an idea, a sentence, even a single word that prompted an impulse to explore further.

The bottom line on these techniques is that you will discover that some work better for you than others. You are constitutionally better suited to some kinds of thought than others. Which could be the motto for the whole writing process if it weren't so clunky. So rather than lock in on a certain approach and feel as if you have to follow it through on *this* project, remember that you didn't take any loyalty oaths to one technique or another. If you try one approach and get stuck, move. Try another one. You'll eventually find one that will get you there. If not, the problem is not with invention techniques but something more basic, like the concept itself or perhaps your attitude (he said from personal experience). Make changes as needed. **Writing, like life, is adjustment.**

How do I know when I'm ready to write?

You'll know. Usually, you begin to write when you can't *not* write. That sounds a little cheerier than it actually is. Yes, sometimes you will be full to bursting with ideas and plans to the point that if you don't start the draft, you'll explode. Or else you just want it off your plate so you can do something other than walk around with the cloud of obligation and guilt hovering over you. But every once in a while, your reason for not writing is that you got stuck with a client presentation at three o'clock in the afternoon and the client is coming tomorrow morning at ten. Or one member (yes, *that* one) of your group project calls the night before to say they just couldn't get their part written, oh well, la-di-da. So even though you now despise that person more than boiled worms for dinner, there is no choice but to write it, given that the entire group's grade rides on successful completion of the project. In that case, your prewriting will be foreshortened. And probably full of bad words. You will, however, be okay, at least if you have made a practice of being mindful about predraft invention. What will happen is that something like muscle memory will take over and you will be inventing madly even as you work your way through the draft. The thing about the writing process is that while practice may not make perfect, it makes better.

This last example illustrates a point composition instructors love to make: **writing is recursive**. Writing gives the impression that it is linear—invention, drafting (beginning, middle, end), revising, and polishing in that order—but that impression is illusory. In fact, the process requires much turning back. "Recursive" derives from a Late Latin word, *recurrere*, meaning "run back," which pretty much fits what we're talking about here. At each stage, the process may send us back to one of the earlier steps. You will get stuck in your draft, which will send you back to the invention stage to develop something you hadn't known then that you would need, or hadn't even realized existed. Revising may cause you to stop and draft a new section before moving forward. Happens to me with alarming frequency. Oddly enough, sometimes the curve is not backward but forward, or even both directions at once. Having drafted the sections of the body of your essay, you may want to stop before writing a conclusion and see if the order of ideas, paragraphs, or arguments in the body makes sense. That sounds a lot like revision even if the draft isn't quite finished. Or maybe you think of that as outlining. I'm okay with that. I often suggest to students that the best time to write an outline is after the draft. The material for the outline is now more fully realized, so it can be clearer, and the act of writing the order out schematically will sometimes lay bare any missteps.

Having given you this extended pep talk about how to start a project, I offer this prediction: within six months or at most a year, you won't do any of these techniques. That does not mean you will skip the invention stage, only that you will internalize the general practice and apply your own approach. Your writing revolves around you from beginning to end. Your knowledge, your thoughts, your personality, your vision. Why would the process itself be any different? It can't be yours if it is imposed from the outside; it can start that way, which is what we do in writing classes, but sooner or later, you need to own it. Indeed, you will want to. Believe me, you'll be happier, not to mention more productive, once you do.

9

Beginnings

*A piece of writing has to start somewhere, go somewhere,
and sit down when it gets there.*
—JOHN MCPHEE

You know what is the hardest thing to do with a piece of writing? Get started. The least fun? Finishing it off. These survey results are based on a sample size of one, but I assume they are universally true. *Wait a minute*, you think, *if starting is so hard, why isn't it the least fun?* Because at the very start, the world of options is wide open. Assuming that you, like me, find your way in from the beginning, you can get going any way you choose. With each succeeding paragraph, your options are increasingly limited, your field of vision narrowed. Sometimes that's helpful, sometimes just annoying.

With any writing project longer than a haiku, we have to get the darned thing going, flesh it out fully, and bring it to an end, gracefully if possible. Come to think of it, the haiku also has three parts, just shorter than most.

A Note on Terminology

Just so you understand, I am going to occasionally use the standard sort of nomenclature about the three phases of writing structure—introduction, body, conclusion—along the way, mostly to avoid stupefyingly frequent repetition. But when you see those three words, I want you to hear "opening, middle, ending." Why? Because those writing-textbook terms are fraught with all sorts of attendant rules and strictures and bad memories. Especially as it concerns "introduction": every textbook I ever looked into (and in the seventies and eighties, they were legion) either offered such tight rules for structure that no room was left for creativity or even thought, or else was so vague as to prove useless.

There are all sorts of advice and orders out there, some helpful and some hideous, for how to shape a piece of writing. Things one must attend to in the opening paragraph (or chapter in the case of books), the shape and content of body paragraphs (or chapters), what one must do and avoid doing in a conclusion. Some of those instructions are presented as recommendations, some as commands, and they vary in tone and message as much as any human communication can. But the real rules are very simple and very scary: the first page needs to make the reader want to read page two, which must build on the first one and impel readers to the next one, and so on until the last, which has a special obligation to make all those preceding pages feel worth all the effort. This pattern is the same whether the item in question is three pages or three hundred. **Keep readers reading.** No one has ever found a simple formula for that challenge, but writers discover myriad ways of accomplishing the task.

In the matter of openings, here's what we're up against. The advice students and others were traditionally given ranged from the mostly serviceable to the nightmarishly prescriptive. Let's start with the second. There was a movement in the not-so-distant past to give student writers marching orders that would carry them through an essay like an army trampling young wheat. The first sentence was the thesis statement of the essay, followed by (in order) the topic sentence of body paragraphs one, two, and three, and culminating either in a restatement of the thesis or a transition into the body of the paper. In the more degraded forms, the thesis actually had a main statement and three subordinate clauses (which is to say, half-sentences that can't stand on their own and are therefore at the service of the main or independent clause, which, owning both a subject and a verb, can stand alone if it wishes to, which in this case it doesn't) detailing the gist of the topic sentences. Just to complete the horror: those topic sentences were the first sentence in each body paragraph and were then repeated in reverse order in the conclusion (from the Latin for, evidently, "it can't get any more boring than this") before the big finish, a restatement of the thesis. And *voilà*, an essay has occurred. In theory. In practice, there is virtually nothing that can be true, beautiful, or good about that form. It is, however, a way of imposing order on the unruly fourteen-year-old brain. It is also easy to grade the resulting "themes." Does each sentence occur in its appointed place(s) in the theme? In the right order? Well, then, we're good, or at least not so bad. Again, in theory.

How do I know such instruction existed? First, because I read some of the texts that ordained it, and second, because I occasionally had those students in class. They were often older than their colleagues in class, meaning they were about my age, and they would cling to that rule-bound form as if their lives depended on it. Helping them break out from that structure was akin to one or possibly two of the labors of Hercules. I encouraged, cajoled, pushed, and once in a while threatened, but the lure of that illusion of structure was so strong that in some cases I never did break through.

Here's the thing about those highly schematic systems: their hearts, or some portion of them, were in the right place. They were attempting to cause students to find a proper starting point and not begin in midargument, thereby leaving readers lost and perplexed. If we consider an opening from a strictly content point of view, it has several tasks. It needs to introduce its subject and give a hint as to what sort of treatment that subject will receive. If you are writing about the coal industry, for instance, will you be arguing to keep it strong, arguing to do away with it as soon as possible, providing an overview of its history and development, discussing its economic role in distressed areas of the country, analyzing the trade-offs between the benefits it brings and damage it inflicts on the environment, or any of a dozen other possibilities? As I write this, a famous and extremely controversial figure in American society has died in the last couple of days. Print and electronic media sources are awash in remembrances that valorize or vilify the man, and every single one of those that I have read strives to make clear right up front just what sort of tack the writer is taking. No one wants their position to be unclear; attitudes toward the subject signal membership in one political tribe or the other. Most of us will never be called upon to identify our position in quite so extreme a fashion, but every introduction must lay out subject and treatment.

In addition to subject and treatment, you are previewing the writer to potential readers. What do you sound like? What sorts of sentences do you write? What is the tone of this work? In other words, who the heck are you and why will anyone feel rewarded if they tag along with you? You and I know there are sound reasons, but you have to show potential readers just what those reasons are. This is where an intro that is wooden or mechanical is a killer. The last thing any of us wants to convey to readers is a message that says: this person is a stiff. I mention elsewhere that John Gardner says that the fiction writer is creating a "vivid and continuous dream" and that anything that breaks that illusion is, literally, a dream-killer. So, too, with the nonfiction writer. What she creates may not be a dream exactly—she's not inviting visitors into a world she has created expressly for this story—but she is trying to welcome them into a space of inquiry, a space she manages efficiently and even entertainingly. Anything at all that breaks that impression of control, from soggy sentences to awkward handling of sources, steals from her efforts. Chief among those impression breakers is an opening that is leaden or clunky. Why? Because you can't simply *tell* readers that you are interesting and have something useful to say; you have to *show* them. If what you show is ineptitude, that will be what they know about you.

In a sense, every piece of writing, and especially every opening of a piece of writing, is an argument with the same message: **read me**. Writers always want to attract and keep readers all the way to the end. At least, that's what they want if they understand the gig. Since I told you what not to do in an opening, it seems only fair that I offer some thoughts on what will work better.

Bait a hook. As the old blues song "Fishin' Blues" tells us, "many fish bite if you got good bait," and that includes the bait we use when writing our *hook*. A hook is the opening sentence, question, claim, assertion, or joke that a writer may use to begin a piece. The idea is that, like fishing, it is intended to draw interest from the intended party whether human or piscine. Here is a hook with bad bait:

> My name is Tom and in this paper I will tell you about the Battle of Asculum.

Notice that there is nothing factually amiss in that sentence. There is also nothing whatsoever to make us want to read another sentence or even find out where Asculum might be. Compare that with this:

> As King Pyrrhus surveyed the carnage after the Battle of Asculum, he received congratulations on the victory from one of his underlings by replying, "Another victory like that and I am done for."

Now that is bait we can work with. We know who was in charge of the battle, the name of the engagement, and within limits, not only that he won but how dearly the victory cost him. In fact, the price was so high that he had to withdraw from the war despite two consecutive victories. The sentence throws us right into the scene with as little mediation (things like "he thought," or "he would later write," or anything of that sort) as possible. It gives us specifics we can work with. In truth, the only thing wrong with that particular gambit is that it has been used a gazillion times. Since the battle was over two thousand years ago, however, even that is almost forgivable.

Whether the word "Asculum" appears or not, some sentence in any piece of writing has to come first, or else none can be second and so on. In journalism, that sentence is called the *lede* (traditionally rendered as *lead*, although since typesetting involves actual lead—with a short "e"—to avoid confusion in print, journalists switched to the above spelling back in the 1970s). There are about as many ways to construct a *lede* as there are ways to construct any other sentence. It can be a statement, a challenge, a question, a presentation of a fact or datum; in fact, it can be anything the writer wants it to be except boring. Remember, we want readers to keep reading. You can begin with a statement, a question, a fact (if sufficiently catchy), a quote (same restriction), a hypothesis, an anecdote, in other words, pretty much anything a sentence can be. There are just two rules one must obey: (1) it must be interesting, and (2) it must be relevant to where this piece of writing is going. You, as the writer, can easily figure out if your lede meets those two criteria, since you are also a reader and can determine interest factor and relevance with assuredness. If you are bored, your readers will be, too, and if you can't figure out the relevance of what you just wrote, what hope is there for anyone else? We'll come back to this magic sentence shortly, but let us first consider what an opening can do besides just lie there inertly.

What should an opening accomplish?

1. Grab readers' attention. Offer the promise of something good. Suggest that the rest of the piece will be worth the effort.

2. Move with something resembling consecutive thought from one point to the next until it arrives at a jumping-off point for the rest of the piece.

3. Provide some notion of the subject and what the essay, article, letter, or whatever this item is will do with that subject.

4. Handle the previous item in a way that sketches, hints at, points toward coming attractions but does not spell them out. That's what the body of the writing is there for.

5. Offer something—an image, a theme, a sentiment, an attitude, a point of contact—that the rest of the piece can return to if the occasion arises. In other words, begin to build some sort of unity.

6. Have a harmony of its own that makes this introductory element feel satisfying in itself while pointing toward a larger purpose that tantalizes readers.

7. Bring your reader to the last sentence of the opening safely and in a condition of wanting to know more. **No one ever reached the end of an essay without reaching the end of the opening.**

Remember what our friend John McPhee said about the purpose of writing? That it "has to start somewhere, go somewhere, and sit down when it gets there." Well, so does an opening, only quicker. It has a beginning, a middle, and an end, often in the space of a single paragraph. How can the writer possibly accomplish all of this? The answer lies in part in being able to keep two things in view at the same time: the prior sentence and the ultimate goal. We know, however, when we try to look in two directions at once, mishaps may occur. I have known more than one friend who, turning to talk to someone behind them while walking down the street, landed on a shoulder. In writing, tripping yourself up rarely results in orthopedic surgery, but communication can be maimed. The best way to banish misfortune is to not look back. Instead, look forward.

Consider how I started this chapter. I began with a question and an answer, or to be strictly accurate, with two consecutive questions and answers: "You know what is the hardest thing to do with a piece of writing? Get started. The least fun? Finishing it off." I followed those with a smart-aleck sort of statement about generalizing from my own experience, and then anticipated a challenge from readers about my claims: "*Wait a minute*, you think, *if starting is so hard, why isn't it the least fun?*" And since even anticipated questions end in question marks, I provided an answer, namely that even if difficult, openings are exciting because of all the freedom they afford the writer. That freedom becomes less with each ensuing choice, until by the end, we are sort of trapped by our own previous decisions. To prove it, I respond to having reduced my own range of options with, "Sometimes that's helpful, sometimes just annoying." At that point, we are ready to launch.

Notice, please, that nowhere in that paragraph is there anything remotely resembling a main idea—because the statement that every piece of writing has a beginning, middle, and ending can hardly be credited with being an idea, much less a "main" one. We will get there in due time. What matters for this discussion is that, with one exception, every sentence grows *directly* out of the one before. The lone outlier is the throwaway joke about the sample size being one, and even that has a connection to the one before and the one after, if only tangentially. Those sentences link up not because I scrambled to always connect back but because in each case, I anticipated where I wanted to go. In sports, whether tennis or basketball or hockey, mediocre players see the play that is currently happening. Decent players think one play ahead, and good ones two. Athletes with pro potential see the game three moves before they happen. I have heard it said that Wayne Gretzky saw the game of hockey four or five moves ahead. There is a reason they call him "the Great Gretzky." You don't have to be a Gretzky—heaven knows that I'm not—to become a competent or even a very good writer, but some level of anticipation is helpful.

Those who are NHL-quality writers can see the future in an opening sentence. Occasionally, the rest of us can have that insight as well. That can be less comforting than it sounds, according to Joan Didion in her *Paris Review* interview: "What's so hard about that first sentence is that you're stuck with it. Everything else is going to flow out of that sentence. And by the time you've laid down the first *two* sentences, your options are all gone." Didion was the last of the major New Journalists, those magazine writers from the sixties who brought the tools of fiction writing to bear on journalistic assignments, and she was the first female to crack that boys' club. Her sentences, first, second, and otherwise, are exquisite. They could be chiseled in stone or cast in bronze. Like Hemingway, whom she resembles on the page, she has absolute control over how much information they release, how much they conceal, and what the silence between them reveals, so if she tells you that your options are gone after the second sentence, you can be bloody well sure that those options are, indeed, kaput.

I differ from Didion not on whether those opening statements are definitive but on the question of their beneficence. She sees the reduction in possibilities as a threat, something that freights those sentences with immense importance and steals from the rest of the article. For me, they point the way to the endzone. Which is part of my credo: **the writer's first goal for a piece of writing is always to move from the initial capital letter to the final period.** Whatever assists in making that journey is a positive to be embraced, whatever hinders it, an ill to be avoided. Put simply, once she can see the end of the article, most of the adventure has gone out of the work, whereas I can see the path through the dark woods to something resembling light.

Let's return to that list of seven requirements for openings. When I was in school, a slightly different model of essay writing had emerged from the wheat-stomping one. This one was sometimes called the hourglass model because the top end went from wide at one end and narrow at the other, while the bottom end went from narrow to wide. The shape resembled, slightly, an hourglass, assuming that the barrel of your hourglass was about a foot long. We'll worry about the barrel and the bottom, inverted funnel a little later, but let's stay focused on the top end. What we were taught was that the *introduction* should begin wide and narrow down to its main point by the end of the paragraph. But how wide is wide? Or too wide? Or not wide enough? We were given a general precept (wide-to-narrow) but no objective way to judge if we were doing it right, nor any suggestions as to how we could use our subjective judgment. Taken to its logical extreme, every essay would begin like a James A. Michener novel: "In the beginning, Creation took place in this location." Seriously, before we could meet any people, we had to see the mountains of Colorado or the islands of the South Pacific rise from the mud or sea. Since Michener novels were about eight million pages each, that is not encouraging for the writer of a four-page essay. What we really need is targeted width: a little wider than the thesis we wish to argue or the analysis we want to pursue, a good bit narrower than the sky.

To accomplish this sort of width, writers should keep their readers in mind. If they can make their lede interesting and relevant, readers will have a sense of direction and a willingness to move ahead. And here is where we give writers more credit than my classmates and I were given all those years ago. If you know yourself and your likely audience, you will understand how much information you need to provide in the lede, and you will see your way from that to your main point. Writers, even comparative beginners, are smart, sometimes downright brilliant. They understand their own reading experience, so they can judge what will work and what won't, which leaps will be too big for their readers and which baby steps are babying readers too much. Most of all, they will understand when boredom becomes a danger (hint: that's most of the time) and figure out how to avoid it.

Exercises

- For an informational article on a subject of your choosing, write at least two different openings. Make them different in substance, not merely in surface features. Can you see different outcomes for the resulting articles?
- For a narrative article on a traumatic event in someone's life, write three openings that employ different moments—one just before, one during, and one significantly after the event. How do they promise to affect what comes afterward in the articles?
- For a personal narrative, write the opening in the first person. Then rewrite it in the third person. If you're feel-

ing bold, write it in the second person, using "you" as if the event is happening to the reader. How does the feel of the thing change from one to another?

Write two versions of the first paragraph of a letter of complaint to a company about a faulty product or customer service procedure. In the first, come across as full-bore angry. In the second, attempt to sound reasonable, but still aggrieved. How do the two make you feel? How do you imagine them being received by the recipient?

The goal, ultimately, is not to come up with umpteen exercises to eat up all your writing time for the next six months but to introduce you to some key questions and the only concept that matters when writing introductions. Questions like: Is this the best place to start? What do I want this to do? Will it appeal to readers? Is the pace right? Is the language inviting? What about the tone? Those questions, and any number of others we might come up with, all fall under a single conceptual umbrella: **an opening must be your best introduction of your subject and treatment to your audience.** Not the best anyone could possibly do; that thinking will tie you in knots before you ever begin. Just *your* best, which is hard enough. That standard requires honesty and discipline about both your performance and your native capabilities. I know people who slough off and always give themselves a pat on the back because "that's pretty good." I also know plenty of perfectionists who aren't capable of perfection (hint: none of us is); they spend their time beating themselves up for not reaching an unattainable standard. Neither evaluation is proper or remotely helpful. **Self-evaluation needs to be not harsh, but just.**

Having begun this chapter with a list of things that must be accomplished in the course of an opening, let's consider some qualities that will help your introduction achieve those aims. They could all be contained in a catchall term, "liveliness." But that doesn't really tell us all that much, does it?

- Intriguing. Readers should be hooked by the first sentence and finish it wanting, demanding to move forward.
- Representative. It should introduce both the subject and treatment and the writer, you.
- Subject-specific. It should carve out one angle of attack from the scores or hundreds possible on the subject.
- Focused. Single-minded, even. It should attempt to do only one thing and do it perfectly.
- Detailed. This is no time to be vague.
- Dynamic. It should suggest *action* in the essay or book or article. Each sentence needs to have a connection to the one before and the one after. To pull one out would be to collapse the whole edifice.
- Fact-laden. It should feel solid, inevitable.
- Verb-dominant. Verbs drive the train; nouns just sit in the seats.
- Flawless. Or as near as you can make it.

See? Nothing to it.

10

The Part Between the Ends

"Begin at the beginning," the King said, gravely, *"and go
on till you come to the end; then stop."*
—LEWIS CARROLL, *ALICE'S ADVENTURES IN WONDERLAND*

"DO YOU WANT THE *body paragraphs from strongest to weakest or
weakest to strongest?*" That is a real sentence, one with which I am
all too familiar. When we would discuss structuring an analysis
of a novel or poem, there was about a fifty-fifty chance that it
would come up. To be sure, the student who asked had good
reason: somewhere between high school English classes and first-
year composition, instructors—people who are supposed to know
these things—imparted diametrically opposed information about
the best way to manage the middle of a paper. In this case, "middle" encompasses everything between the end of the opening and
the start of the ending, which can be anything from a couple of
pages to ninety-five percent of a book. That pretty well embodies
the term "loose definition." Since I knew the question was at least
possible, I had an answer ready: "I want them in the best possible

order." They often received my wisdom with eye rolls and sighs of exasperation. It's good to be appreciated.

I was not, however, just messing with them. My point, which I always hastened to explain, was that neither of those ways of ordering the development of an essay guaranteed anything like a best outcome.

At a very early stage of writing instruction, probably around late middle school, the best-to-worst-or-vice-versa organizational method makes sense, but not because it will produce better essays. What it really teaches students is to dispassionately evaluate the quality of their work: Which parts of my argument are strong and which ones less so? Self-evaluation is a skill that is not only useful in life but takes most of a lifetime to perfect. I'll let you know when I master it. Sooner or later, though, and I recommend sooner, students need to move past that sort of hierarchy in their writing.

Since you and I are mostly reasonable and mostly grown-up, we can advance our thinking on writing organization. Discussions of beginnings and endings are pretty straightforward: an opening is the writing equivalent of an airplane going from a standstill on the runway to lifting off and reaching cruising altitude; an ending reverses the process, safely returning from hurtling through the sky to standing quietly at the terminal. Takeoffs and landings can be smoother or rougher, but the nature of each is common to all flights. What transpires in between, however, fills vastly more time and miles than the first two combined. And that's the part that interests us here. Seen from the outside, the bulk of air travel looks like nothing much, just a matter of keeping the plane aloft, and how hard can that be? For the persons in the cockpit, on the other hand, there are hundreds of details big and small that must be attended to maintain altitude, stay on course, arrive at the destination on time, and avoid any midair unpleasantness. And without attention to those details, well, let's just say they must be attended to.

So it is with writing. The middle, the body, whatever we want to call it, is the part that does nearly all the work but gets too little of the applause. Not only that, even our language about it is dismissive—compare the big sound of "introduction" and "conclusion" with "the body" and tell me it gets held in the same esteem. Somehow, we tend to think of it as this thing to be got through so we can tie everything up in a bow with an ending. Yet it stands between and is vastly longer than those two endpoints, so we can hardly expect to simply leap over all that intervening effort. As with air travel, there is much work to be done in and on "the middle."

Work, yes, but what? And how? Every middle game is different—in structure, in intent, in pacing, in outcomes, in certainty. At the short end of the writing spectrum, the middle is chiefly manageable. If you are writing a three-page personal essay consisting of five or so paragraphs, it will be hard for organization to get away from you. Even if it does, you can wrestle paragraphs into a different order with ease. Seeing the logic that drives your choices will be a snap. But with each increase in length, everything becomes harder. At ten pages, the writer inevitably has more questions about navigating through the forest without running into trees. At twenty, certainty diminishes; at thirty, it all but vanishes on a first run-through. At book length, lotsa luck. As an undergraduate, I became something of an expert in writing five-to-seven-page essays, not because I was gifted at them but merely because they were assigned in pretty much every course I took. Outlines weren't needed, especially after the first few. My classmates and I knew what they looked like, what they needed to contain, what their rhythm was; what we did was more or less plug-and-play (long before the term came into vogue), substituting the idea for this essay for whatever the idea had been in the last one and then grinding out the pages. But then I got a big shock with my final senior seminar paper (twelve to fifteen pages) and my senior thesis (sixty, with chapters). Oh, my! Twelve pages may not sound all that much longer than seven, but you can't get there simply by puffing up a seven-pager. The strategies are different. The idea needs to be bigger, the scope wider or deeper. Or both. This one turned out to require more planning, which meant dusting off the outlining techniques I had first encountered in fifth or sixth grade. My fellow seminarians had much the same experience. The thesis required even more strategic thinking about chapter contents and order, scale of the idea (obviously bigger than the seminar paper, but by how much?), plans to maintain cohesiveness, and a dozen other concerns.

All of these issues can be managed. At the time, it seemed that I just felt my way forward to longer formats, but it turned out that wasn't quite accurate. Once there was time for reflection, I realized that I had spent four years reading literary criticism in the form of journal articles and book chapters, and these longer forms had seeped into my consciousness. It would be quite difficult, of course, to perform an act one has never observed, but I had witnessed numerous such performances. Reading is valuable to the writer! Who knew?

Writers have a good deal of latitude in how they arrange their writing, regardless of genre. Not even autobiography and memoir require strict adherence to an imposed order, in their cases, to chronology. You might think so, given that we experience life from beginning to end following the march of time, but that's just living, and we're talking writing here. Don't misunderstand; there is nothing wrong with narrating an event you experienced or even your entire remembered existence in the order in which it happened. Many persons have done that quite successfully. But you don't have to. For instance, if you are telling your life as one of conversion from selfish misbehavior to virtuous generosity, and if there is a key event that caused or expressed that pivot, you might just want to begin with that moment. You might then flash back and start from the beginning. Or perhaps not. For aesthetic or intellectual or thematic reasons, you might do better to hop-scotch around in time so that you can build the theme of misdeeds and redemption. Timelines, you see, are not always friendly to construction of ideas. Events are dictated by our actions as we move through time, and those events and our responses to them influence how our character develops. In a piece of writing, on the other hand, we are not building our character but choosing how best to reveal it based on a host of independent factors that can drive our structure. Aesthetics is one such basis: How can I tell this so that it provides the most pleasure or seems the most attractive? Intellectual consideration is another: How best can I use this material to make my point or elucidate my theme? Narrative drive can be another: How swiftly do I want the story to move by, or how much suspense do I want to build into the telling? If you begin with the moment of change, that will likely dissipate a good deal of suspense. If you use a hopscotch structure, readers may be slowed down as they figure out where in the story they are or what means you're employing to keep them from being lost.

Every writing decision, you see, is a trade-off. If you decide to write a novel using an omniscient narrator, meaning one who has a godlike perspective and can be everywhere in the novel and know what every character is thinking, your narrator will be the master of information, knowing everything he can possibly know. That comes, though, with a couple of problems. First, you can't hide anything. If you discover in chapter thirty-two that it is inconvenient to reveal the villain's motivation, tough luck; your narrator can't suddenly develop amnesia, being godlike and all. That's a big issue but not the worst. Or biggest. All that knowing everything really adds up. Don't be shocked if your novel is eight hundred pages long. It turned out thus with some regularity for the Victorians.

Organization

To think of the *DEVELOPMENT* or *body* of a piece of writing as the middle is to deny it credit. For one thing, there's the matter of length. A five-paragraph essay may only have three paragraphs in its body because when we subtract two paragraphs from five, we arrive at a small number. Consider, however, what happens when we subtract the opening and closing chapters of a book that has thirty-five chapters (oh, relax, this one has nowhere close to that). We are left with thirty-three chapters of "middle" (again, not the case here). Even if we allow a couple of chapters to launch and then land the book, that still leaves thirty-one. Based on the numbers involved with books, we need to rethink our understanding of development in nonfiction, but it is no less true for shorter essays and articles. When submitting a query for an article or a book proposal, writers need to address what are sometimes called the "four Ps": Problem, Promise, Program, and Platform. The Problem is the reason that the piece of writing is needed, whether that is some social ill or a story the public would be better off knowing. The Promise is the assertion that the writer can correct the problem by informing, analyzing, or explaining. The Program addresses the specific means that the writer will use to fulfill the Promise. The Platform, finally, is the qualifications the writer brings that make him, her, or them uniquely capable of achieving these aims. Of these four, the only one of those that doesn't get addressed in the body of a work is the *platform*, the writer's credentials to do this work. The others, though, only find their real home in the development. The writer has to establish that the *problem* is legitimate. She then has to not only articulate the *promise* again (and again and again as she moves through a long piece of writing) because readers have shortish memories, but move forward and not only express but accomplish the *program* in considerable detail. Put another way, she needs to establish that her point is valid and that it is worth making, which is an ongoing process throughout the duration of the work, however long it may be. Think of writing as a form of chess, where openings can be a handful of moves (some *gambits*, where a piece is sacrificed to gain advantage later on, announce themselves in a single move), with endgames sometimes just as brief, like lightning strikes that deliver victory. In this scenario, the middle game is anywhere from considerably to vastly longer than openings and endgames.

Because of this disparity of length, the main body of a work is where the writer's organizational skills and devices really come into play. Which part comes before which other parts? Which goes last? Why? How do I stitch these pieces together to suggest more connection between them than might be evident on their own? In other words, here is where your outline or whatever you use in place of one really earns its paycheck. And the longer a piece of writing is, the harder it is to keep all those balls in the air. In a four-page student essay, while having a bad organization of the middle section is certainly possible, there isn't all that much room to go too far wrong. And if the writer arrives at the end and sees that the middle is all wrong, it doesn't take too much labor to reorder all the bits. Change that writing to a twenty-five-page graduate term paper, though, and the possibilities for mayhem approach the infinite.

How we think about our readers will govern how we go about developing the middle game of our writing. The more fully we understand the audience's needs, the better we can envision what we must do to address those needs. What, then, are the baseline requirements of readers?

- Readers hate feeling lost. Ever. The writer has to keep their feet on solid ground.
- Readers want a structure that makes sense to them, which is to say, they want the writer to explain the logic of the organization and method of proceeding.
- Readers need clarity. That means clarity of ideas and of presentation.
- Readers demand proof. Every assertion a writer makes needs to be backed up by evidence, often by more than one piece of evidence. We can have too little evidence but rarely too much.
- Readers need explanation. Providing both a *claim* and a *ground* (the evidence part of the program) is not enough.

The writer must make the connection between the two clear through explanation (the Toulmin model's *warrant*).

Brass Tacks

WHETHER THREE PAGES OR THREE hundred, the part between the ends is constructed with the same building blocks as the introduction and ending: sentences and paragraphs. The difference is that that long parade of paragraphs must work as something approaching a continuous entity. Openings? Not so much. They tend to begin with some noisy stratagem to garner attention, build on that device for a bit, and then announce a grand plan while handing off responsibility for developing that to the next part. Job done. Endings attempt to tie up the frayed threads of all that has gone before and tie those into a pleasing bow that leaves readers with a satisfied feeling that the job has been accomplished. In other words, they are the prima donnas of the written word. If writing were football, they'd be wide receivers. And the middle? Offensive linemen, doing all the hard work for no glory and little credit, only blame when things go wrong.

Well, then, how does the writer make sure things don't go wrong? Planning. Blocking out the big movements is what an outline or equivalent does for writers of longer works. If you are writing very short pieces, you'll be done before you can outline anything, so skip over that. That said, anytime you can think of a piece of writing in terms of bigger chunks, you will do well to lay it out schematically according to some system that makes sense to you and that you won't forget over time. Outlines are taught in schools because they work, yes, but also because the system is pre-existing, so no invention is required. Another plus: when a student moves to a different school whether through graduation or transfer, the basics of outlining will be the same. There is something to be said for ubiquity. But it isn't a system that seems to produce results for everyone, so if you are one of "not everyone," do something else to assist your planning stage. The nonfiction writer John McPhee writes his ideas on note cards so that he can arrange them not only in any order but in any design he wishes. He works in a circular narrative in his book *Coming into the Country* (1976), and having laid out his cards in a circle, he picks a spot that is chronologically neither first nor last to begin his narrative. Try that with an outline! I do follow outlines, which chiefly look like—and sometimes remain—chapter titles. Those chapters that actually come to pass frequently get moved around as I look for the most satisfying arrangements. Occasionally, they move not just within a section of the book but to a different section entirely. Sometimes, alas, they get cut altogether. But chapters are merely one of an array of options. My old friend and writing group colleague John Smolens wrote his first novel, *Winter by Degrees* (1988), in sheafs of about five pages, not because of some numerical fascination but because his personal computer at the time was, if I have this straight after many years, a Commodore 64, and with its tiny processor and tinier random-access memory, it could hold no more writing in a file before it had to be saved to a floppy disk and a new "document" begun. Most chapters were around ten pages, so about two files per chapter. That wouldn't be too hard to move chapters, so long as one remembered to move both files. Besides being a tale of perseverance overcoming technological shortcomings, this is a reminder that we are living in a better part of the computer age. If you don't know what a floppy disk was, count your blessings and ask your parents. Or grandparents.

There is also, of course, planning on a micro scale. If you want your work to flow from paragraph to paragraph, you need to plan at a different level. The ability to see the next two or three pages is useful. If you can't, then you can't, although it might be something that you can work on. What makes this visionary quality matter so much? Just this: if the goal of writing the middle of a piece is continuity, then the writer must devote attention to more than the current sentence. To do that is, like the player who only sees the play as it happens, to be always behind the ball and chasing to catch up. If the piece in question is a class newsletter, then continuity counts for a lot less than in an essay, since each news item (with the classmate's name coming at or very near the top of the paragraph) is a freestanding tidbit with its own *raison d'être*. For most writing tasks, however, continuity matters, imperfect though it be. Nor is it only *this sentence right here* that we must see beyond. The same applies to paragraphs. Knowing when you write a paragraph what will come next, and then the one after and the one after that and the one after that (while recalling what came just before), will prove invaluable in holding things together on the local level. In this way, the writer can adjust the current paragraph so that it anticipates what will be said even while saying what needs to be here and now.

I wrote the previous paragraph about an hour before the one before it, after my friend's novel but before the planning bit. I suddenly saw that *that* one would have to make an appearance somewhere, although whether in one more paragraph or five I didn't know. But knowing that I would write it eventually told me that I should write it now, then double back and find my way forward to it. This is not because I'm some kind of genius (I have by this point amply demonstrated otherwise) but because my thinking is erratic in ways that occasionally, although not always, work out in my favor.

We will talk about sentences and paragraphs in more detail elsewhere. For the moment, we are concerned not with assembling them but with thinking strategically about them. *Why this order? Why not that one? Let's try that one and see. No, definitely not that one. Still, is this one the best I can do?* The order of middle paragraphs—or sentences or pages or chapters—is driven partly by logic and partly by feel. And even "feel" is probably logic of a sort, since what you feel usually grows out of your intent, even when that may be something subconscious that you can't at the moment articulate. Writers usually "know" what they're doing, which is why the parts of a writing project tend to fall into place, and if they don't, those parts can be rearranged without too much fuss because in the course of writing the failed version, one or more alternatives will present themselves. The single greatest boon to society of the computer age isn't IBM's Watson or sending rovers to Mars; it's the cut-and-paste feature of word processors.

Knowing how you will proceed broadly makes what happens with individual paragraphs and sentences manageable. Let's think of a paragraph as having four phases. The first is the opening gambit, that transition or other bit of language, often merely a word or phrase, that leads into the first sentence. That sentence is typically the *anchor* for the rest of the paragraph, stating a claim or asking a question that will drive what happens thereafter. The generic term that you will have used in class will be "topic sentence," a sort of mini–thesis statement. The trouble is, not every first sentence boldly states the topic for the paragraph—nor does every paragraph need one. But every paragraph needs something to get it started, a sort of anchor to which it can tether the rest. The third and longest phase will be the expansion and explanation and support of that anchor, the "body" of the paragraph. The fourth phase, unsurprisingly, is a concluding statement, because every paragraph needs an exit strategy. Would it surprise you to find that there are at least four ways to connect paragraphs: transitional material at the beginning, anchor statements that tie into previous material, echoes of earlier language anywhere in the paragraph body, and pre-transitional material at the end? Didn't think so. There may be more, but these seem to cover most instances.

Each of these points of connection begs for elucidation. I dislike the word "transition" when connected with paragraphs because it conjures up images of the dreaded *sentence adverb*—"Sadly," "Conversely," "Honestly," "Clearly"—dreaded because they are so weak as transitions and because once students learn of their existence, they try to employ them as solutions to all transitional needs. There are all sorts of ways to shift from one paragraph to the next. The first noun clause of this paragraph, "Each of these points of connection," does just that without any overt "transition-here flags" attached. Does hedging my bet by speaking of "transitional material" solve anything? Probably not, but it makes it harder for readers to file away as "some-word-with-'-ly'"-appended.

That undefined "material" may be a reference to the content of the previous paragraph or to some statement even earlier that makes the tie-in between this new paragraph and previous ones clear. Such references may well be a constituent part of the anchor sentence, as in my example just now, without up-front signals like, "Hopefully," thank goodness. That word suffers enough abuse already.

The body sentences have their own important work to do in buttressing the anchor statement and building toward some sort of payoff, but they can also draw connections to earlier material. In fact, they can be better places to refer to something earlier than just the prior paragraph because they are just far enough removed as to seem free from such a tight connection. Whenever sentences talk back and forth across paragraphs—without sounding contrived or forced—that's a good sign for continuity, since clearly there are threads running through the piece.

Whatever doubts I have about "transitions," they pale in comparison with those of my own "pre-transitional material." Still, I needed some sort of shorthand for what happens in excellent final sentences, which offer up a phrase or word or thought that can act as a springboard to the next paragraph. This is a one-sided conversation I had regularly with my literature students about their even having concluding sentences. When writing about literature, there is necessarily a good deal of paraphrasing and quoting the works in question. Students often mistake those quotes for having proved their point. They would have a perfectly sensible topic sentence, an explanatory sentence or two, and then a quote (sometimes half a page, because what beefs up a paper more than needlessly long quotes?), and then a paragraph break. Here's roughly how this would go:

Me: What makes you think you're done here?
They: I said everything I had to say.
Me: And the quote?

They: It explains everything! There's nothing more to say.

Me: So fictional or poetic words can only be interpreted one way?

They: Um . . .

Those of you who have read literature will know that stories and poems and such rarely have only one meaning, only one way they can be read. Those of you who have taught or explained anything to anyone also know that there is no human utterance that some listener can't misconstrue inadvertently or maliciously. Forty years in front of classes taught me that there is no such thing as a simple declarative sentence. Every utterance can be misheard by someone. How much easier, then, to take a different meaning from words that have ambiguity and nuance baked into them? You must nail down exactly what that passage means to you. Your readers may not agree, but at least they will be clear on your intent: finish your check, as they say in hockey.

There is a second reason to see your paragraph's argument through. The first responsibility of the next paragraph is to find a way to tie itself to the one before, so as you are writing the one before, it behooves you to ease that task. It is vastly easier to prepare the way with your own language than to strain to make a connection to Wordsworth's quatrain. It is shocking how little creative writers care about the continuity needs of later critics. Shameful, really.

Look, I was once one of "they," too. I would find the perfect quote and promptly drop the mic. I had done my work, so why couldn't I count on a little help from my readers? But the truth was that I hadn't done my work, part of which was leading the reader toward my conclusions. What wised me up? Philosophy classes. You want a wake-up call? Leave an argument unfinished in an essay on David Hume. One of the benefits of my teachable moment was that I found that it was far easier to lock an argument together if I constructed the building blocks myself. I think you will also discover that benefit, possibly without needing to rewrite your Hume paper.

Not every paragraph will have all these parts. A "paragraph" can be a sentence fragment or even single word made to stand out all alone as a sort of punctuation for what has gone before:

"As if!"

We are speaking here, however, of the garden-variety get-us-to-the-end-of-this-essay paragraph. Those rhetorical johnny-jump-ups don't come into play here. The stock answer to "How many sentences should a paragraph contain?" is three to five, the logic seeming to be that shorter than that and it's not really doing its job and longer ones go to pieces and lose their singular focus in the hands of student writers. As you can imagine, these are not rigid limits. If you stray over the line and add a sixth or ninth sentence, the paragraph police do not come and arrest you. If, on the other hand, in writing those extras you stray off the topic of the paragraph, those same cops may show up with handcuffs and red pencils. You don't want that.

11

Endings

The perfect ending should take the reader slightly by surprise and yet seem exactly right to him. He didn't expect the article to end so soon, or so abruptly, or to say what it did. But he knows it when he sees it. Like a good lead, it works.

—WILLIAM ZINSSER

A COUPLE OF CHAPTERS ago, I gave you a reason that writing endings can be a drag. Here's another: by the time some of us reach that stage, we kind of lose interest. The heavy lifting was done earlier. As I mentioned, I always worked so hard on writing introductions in college that, when the time came to wrap up, I was exhausted. And often out of time, with another paper to start. What wound up appended to my essays was perfunctory at best. Right: not a great role model.

Over the years, I came to see that there was another thought hiding behind the tiredness: I felt like everything had been said and that the conclusion was self-evident. I just wanted to write a paragraph the entirety of which was "QED" for *quod erat demonstrandum*, meaning "which was to be demonstrated." It wasn't true; nothing had been demonstrated. Oh, I had pursued my arguments to their last point. I had adduced evidence in support of my claims and explained how the two parts nestled together. I had done everything. Except finish the bloody thing. In retrospect, I see that my conduct was not only self-defeating, it was rude to readers. Having demanded their attention for a number of pages, I owed them a debt that could only be repaid by bringing those pages to a satisfying ending so that the matter did indeed feel demonstrated.

It is worth remembering that everybody, absolutely *everybody*, has trouble with endings. Poets, essayists, biographers, historians, novelists. Especially novelists. Here is one of the greats, E. M. Forster, on the difficulty of tying off a novel: "In the losing battle that the plot fights with the characters, it often takes a cowardly revenge. Nearly all novels are feeble at the end. This is because the plot requires to be wound up" (*Aspects of the Novel*, 1927). Perfectly good characters, even excellent ones, are sacrificed at the altar of getting the writer out of the blasted book. Think of poor Huck Finn once Tom Sawyer shows up to torment Jim and wreck everything the book has been teaching us for so long. Short stories are easier to end, since there isn't time for the plot to ball itself up into a Gordian knot. Story endings are almost always cleaner and more satisfying than those of their longer kin.

Historians and biographers may have it slightly easier. Lives, like historical events and eras, end. A chronological endpoint, however, is not the same as a narrative one, and even they must craft an intellectually satisfying finish to this narrative they have created over many, many pages. But they have to do so while limited by those tricky devils, facts. And poets have been known to simply punt, settling for some cryptic statement that gets them out of the morass they have wandered into, although it may leave readers unsettled. William Butler Yeats solved many of his thornier poetic difficulties exactly this way. A novelist usually can't escape so easily.

To be sure, the problems of the novelist are not those of most of us, tasked as we are with writing some variety of nonfiction. But we, also, suffer, if less artistically. On the other hand, we don't have easy culprits like plot and character not making nice. As a result, there is no one to blame but ourselves.

That doesn't mean that we give up or give in. There are ways to craft the best ending possible—again, by understanding the writer-audience relationship and the needs of each side—to make the task as satisfying as it can be. Let's say for the sake of argument that you, as writer, have known what you have been up to throughout the essay or narrative right up to the ending. That is to say, you have been clear about the writer's will throughout. Arriving at the last of the body (or the end of the middle of the paper), you likely know what you want to see happen in your final paragraph. To get there, though, you have to immerse yourself in minds far less clear to you, those of your readers. Here is the payoff for having developed a clear image of your audience at the outset. If you have done that, you will find it easier to envision what they need at this point. What questions likely remain for them? What confusions might have arisen that you need to address? What might they find satisfying as a finale? The answers to these and any other questions will drive construction of your ending.

It is one thing to talk about the psychosocial interaction that will impel your conclusion, but another to translate that abstract understanding into practical action. There's no point in hammering the old five-paragraph-theme advice further. Suffice it to say that in the worst models, the writer was to restate the topic sentence of each body paragraph (in most versions, in reverse order) and then tack on some final concluding bromide or, worse, a restatement of the thesis. Ick. Read a bunch of professional articles and essays and see if that's what happens. Heck, just read the endings. Let me know how often they follow that advice. Much of the available advice follows a similar script. Those collegiate writing labs that maintain websites walk their students through a fairly programmatic series of steps, which will produce a suitable conclusion to a college essay, if not exactly radiant writing. What's missing? An understanding on the part of the writer of the purpose of those steps in terms of writer and audience. Every collection of instructions I have ever read on the subject of conclusions hits the same points. With a few exceptions, they strike me as sterile and lackluster. And don't readers deserve, after bearing with the writer all this time, a little luster?

If that's not the way to go, what is? Rather than offer strict rules, let's lay out a handful of principles.

- First of all, remember that not only the entire piece of writing has a beginning, middle, and ending; so does each component.
- By way of transition, connect to the previous paragraph, the preceding section. Pick up some thread, some theme that you closed your main argument with.
- Reacquaint readers with the importance of your discussion of this topic. That should grow out of the thread you

just took up. You can accomplish this positively, by leaning into your argument, or negatively, by mentioning deficiencies in the counterargument of detractors. Or both.

- Review, don't repeat. Remind readers of where you have taken them (and why) while avoiding a verbatim rehash of sentences they have already seen. No one cares to hear the same thing over and over. Briefly recall the salient points.

- Synthesize, don't summarize. Pull those significant elements into an overarching understanding. While it is true that you don't want to introduce new arguments or facts in a conclusion, that doesn't mean you can't bring a clearer understanding of them.

- Finish with a statement that makes your final point really feel final. Don't oversell it by claiming that this change in village policy will cure cancer or end world hunger—unless it will. Stick to the topic at hand but make it feel finished and satisfying.

How to accomplish all this? There is good news and bad news here, as with so much. There are a thousand paths to your personal waterfall, but no one can tell you ahead of time which path is best for this particular journey. If you have been listening to yourself as you have built your piece, you will know by now how to proceed. Remember that bit back when we discussed openings and the advantage of playing a move or two ahead? Here is where that advice really comes into play. Most successful endings display some sort of awareness of what has gone before them, some part of the piece that they can fold back onto in a semblance of symmetry. You can make that awareness easier to demonstrate if, during the body of your piece, you consciously laid the ground-work for this big finish. If you did not, all is not lost. You can still go through and hunt for the points of connection to harken back to in your conclusion. It is just easier if you can build in those connections as you go. That's a slightly higher-order skill and comes with practice and time.

Sometimes, the difficulties we encounter with endings do not lie in them but elsewhere. There are several issues that occur earlier in the writing that can compromise endings. One is when the essay or paper or article contradicts itself, making it difficult for a conclusion to bring the threads together. If threads clash, it is difficult to bring harmony.

In situations like this, the conclusion can be a useful diagnostic tool for examining the rest of the paper. If the ending just won't come, it may indicate that the earlier parts of the piece do not align with each other. Whenever we write, we need to be alert to hints and allegations that something is amiss. If, for instance, you find it impossible to write a transition from one paragraph to the next, they may have nothing to say to each other. Or do but haven't been on speaking terms. That is correctable, but not by writing a better transition. In this case, if your big finish won't let itself be written, maybe the body of the work isn't ready for finishing. **In any case, always listen to your writing; it is talking to you with every word you write.** And it doesn't like being ignored.

There are ways to learn to listen, but one of the best is to perform a postmortem after the draft. As I have said earlier, I am ambivalent about outlines (shh, don't tell your writing teacher). I see their value as devices for imposing order on unruly minds, and they can sometimes help some people plan out their work.

But I have also seen it cripple other writers who need to feel their way into their topic. But here is where I absolutely believe in an outline: after the first draft is finished. If you write one in advance, you can stray off it as you go, but if you compile an outline afterward, you've already strayed, so you can identify where you went wrong (also right, which is helpful). A lot of people would be shocked how easy it is to finish a piece of writing and not *really* know what you said in it. The easiest—and sometimes the last—chance to catch that problem and fix it is once the first draft is done. Once you revise and leave the vexing spots unchanged, your sense that things are as they should be begins to grow and harden, making it increasingly difficult to alter.

Of the three phases of a piece of writing, endings stand alone as the spot where writers can see the whole picture. The opening needs to address the work it hopes to initiate, but that work has yet to materialize. Once we begin developing the middle phase, the body, the focus is single-minded: this is the thing that must happen right here, in this paragraph. Middles are frequently case studies in tunnel vision. Only when the development has taken place is there a vantage point from which to survey the entire scene. Writers need to juggle that overarching vision with the immediate demands of each sentence, to keep things moving while holding back the impulse to race toward the finish line, to produce a complete utterance but avoid bloating and redundancy. Is it any wonder they drive us crazy?

12

Don't Edit a Flying Leap

*I can write better than anyone who can write faster, and
I can write faster than anyone who can write better.*
—A. J. LIEBLING

MANY YEARS AGO, MY wife and I were standing in what had been our attic, midway through removing the roof before framing a second story on our ranch-style home, when we looked out to the street and saw our blue Ford Escort wagon back out of the driveway and pull away. Since the only two experienced drivers in the house were *on* it, only two solutions presented themselves: ghosts and thieves. Then we remembered that there was another driver at our address, our newly licensed sixteen-year-old son. But while he had passed his driver's test, he had never soloed, so that moment was a little unnerving. It transpired that he had a guitar lesson and we had not moved quite to his satisfaction, so he took the initiative and the Escort. What really happened was that he was ready, and more than ready, to prove himself, and would not be contained a second more.

Writing is a little like that: a moment arrives when all the preparations have been made and the writer can't hold back from composing a draft any longer. All that planning and note taking and scheming have reached a point where they clash and bash into each other inside the brain and have to find expression. *Now*. Or, in many cases, the deadline is bearing down and will not take "no" for an answer. Never discount the power of anxiety as a motivator—or as an inhibitor. When that moment announces itself, so does the trouble. For many of us, getting started is the hardest part. Actually, the hardest part is getting out of our own way. So many rules, so many teachers' voices in our ears, so many things that can go wrong. How do we overcome all that? Write like a bat out of hell. Jump off the cliff. Let go and fly. And for heaven's sake, don't even consider editing a word. That is for later.

In order to make that start, to write something, anything, even if it isn't Hemingway's "one true sentence," the writer has to understand one basic truth: drafts are not meant to be perfect. They exist so that they can come to great harm, from violent editing to total rewriting and even to winding up in trash cans or files.

The novelist, memoirist, and writing guru Anne Lamott offers the pithiest advice: write sh***y first drafts. By all means, do just that. Sh***y can be fixed. Confused can be fixed. Aimless can be fixed. **Any draft can be fixed except one that doesn't exist.** That isn't original with me or Lamott or anyone I know. Every writing instructor who has ever instructed has said or shown the importance of getting a draft on paper or parchment or vellum or computer screen. The word "fixed" as I have used it here means "edited," and you can edit an actual draft. You must, therefore, create one. And be quick about it. The goal of a first draft is not to be publishable but to give you something to work on.

Most experts on writing prefer the quick but imperfect approach to drafting. Here are a couple of instances. My late friend Jim Cash, who wrote *Top Gun*, among other movies, had a process involving a locked door and a weekend. He would shut himself away for a weekend and write what he called a *blast*. It was kind of like a screenplay in that there was dialogue and exposition, but no screenplay in the history of movies had so many repetitions and variants of "I don't know." Whenever he reached a sticking place, which was every few pages, he would simply admit he didn't know what happened next and move on to the next thing he did know. Sometime on Sunday or early Monday, he would stumble out of his writing room looking the worse for wear (although he did not drink) with something like 60 pages. A finished screenplay for a two-hour movie is about 120 pages, so 60 sounds like half, right? No such chance. Most of the blast never made the final script, but it was something to work on and develop. He would share the results with his writing partner, Jack Epps Jr., and off they would go, Jack in Hollywood and Jim in East Lansing, Michigan. This was pre-internet, so the phone bills must have been phenomenal.

The second tale falls under the heading of unlikely sources. My longtime dentist asked what I was working on, and when I told him, he offered this story:

> I've always been a terrible speller, which slowed down my writing when I was a kid. But then in high school I had a great English teacher, Mrs. W., who told me to write my first drafts as fast as I could with no pausing for spelling or anything else. That really freed me up to get something on paper, and *something* can be fixed, but *nothing* can't be.

That sounds like something we've heard elsewhere, doesn't it? We are somewhere very near consensus about the importance of writing a draft, but also with the relative lack of importance of the *quality* of that draft. **Compose, then repair, never the reverse.** I mean, if you can't trust your dentist, then who can you trust?

The reality of drafting stands in contrast with the myth of writing. How many times have writers been shown crumpling up sheet after sheet of paper and tossing them if not into the wastebasket, at least in its approximate direction? And then some psychological bell sounds, and the writer whips off a finished document that emerges from the typewriter letter-perfect. The myth is so appealing that I almost wish my laptop produced sheets of paper for me to crumple. There's just one thing: **it doesn't work that way.** Oh, the failures represented by those balls of paper are real enough. We all have plenty of false starts, fumbles and stumbles, and frustrated outbursts on the tortuous path to a first draft. The untrue part is what that draft actually looks like. Which is a mess. There may be less spilled ink on modern drafts produced via computer, but there are gaps left to indicate material still needed, along with highlighted passages that need concerted attention, and dozens of things that aren't notated as trouble but are trouble nonetheless. I'd like to drive a stake through the heart of that story.

Along the same lines, the bane of every student writer's existence is the legend of the first-draft master, the mythic creature, usually on another floor of the dorm or in some friend's fraternity house (rarely one's own), who sits down the night before a paper is due and writes single-draft papers that invariably get A grades, except when a plus is appended. At my institution, the tale was improved by adding that this phenomenon could accomplish his feats after spending the front half of the evening lubricating the mental machinery with alcohol. That guy (or gal) makes everyone else feel just so inadequate. Kind of what urban legends do. Why "legend" and "myth"? Because, with incredibly rare exceptions, those miracles of nature don't exist. To be sure, the person in question is real enough. In our case, he had a name and a specific campus address on frat row. Still, here's why we needn't feel envy or inadequacy or any of those self-destructive sensations: we cannot see inside their brains, so we lack a view of their process.

So how do they do it? Most of them have a process that may be as involved as anything taught in a composition class, but it is all internal—the prewriting or invention stage, the organization, even the drafting and revising and editing. And because they don't have to stop for cross-outs or backspace-deletes, they can work through their process at high speed. With practice, this sort of internalized process can even proceed while the conscious brain is engaged in other high-level functions, like ordering lunch or playing softball. What an observer will see, then, is not a first draft but a final one. The accomplishment is still impressive even if less magical than the legend would have it. I don't discount the possible existence of a Mozart of writing, someone from whom perfectly formed sentences and whole essays simply pour, but the likelihood is small.

After all, how many Mozarts has music produced?

How, then, does one write a draft like a bat out of hell? The first, and most critical, element is preparation. You can't write quickly if you're fumbling for ideas, for logic, for a plan. That means you must lay the foundation in your preparatory phase, that part we called "invention" a few pages back. Call it "prewriting" if you must, but you know my thoughts on that. With that done, give yourself the best chance to write swiftly. Get rid of distractions to the extent that you can. Turn off the television. Music is okay, but radio with a lot of talk is lousy. The only voices you want to hear are the ones in your head. If you live with other people and you can't kick them out—and who can?—find a quiet space. When my family was young and we lived in a small ranch house, I wrote in a finished room in the basement. Not everyone has one of those, so you may have to create your space with noise-canceling headphones.

Guidelines for Swift Drafting

- Prepare (mental). Do your due diligence on the invention phase. Know your plan, your idea structure, your organization. Keep your outline in easy reach.
- Prepare (physical). Keep your workspace ready for work. Don't have extraneous items in the way that have to be cleared out or have your desk double as your fly-tying bench (those feathers will tickle your nose). Try to reduce chances of interference by having a space without traffic. If you work better with music, choose material that doesn't tempt you to sing along. If everything makes you sing along, play Vivaldi or Mozart.
- Before you take a break for lunch or overnight, try to leave yourself cues that will start the process, like sentences that you know how to finish. It helps to prime the pump.
- Get rid of distractions. Turn off phone notifications. There's a sentence that never existed before about 2005. Or needed to.

- Stick to your task. Your goal here is to create a draft, not to check your email or create a grocery list.

- Be single-minded about the job at hand, but open to options within it. Be aware that there may be more ways to proceed than the one you started with. If you think of a second opening paragraph, write it and mark it as such. Leave decisions about which is best until later.

- *Never get stuck!* We all do, but don't let that stop you. If you don't know what to say next about a point, write a name for the point, highlight it, and move on to the next point. If there's a section you can't see yet, write something like, "Don't know what goes here," and highlight in bright blue or screaming yellow. I compose on my laptop and use the highlight feature in Word, but if you write with pen or pencil, use an actual highlighter. Sometimes I just highlight the last sentence written and leave white space after it; I've come to know what that means.

- Fix nothing. Keep going. Feel free to leave notes in the margin, but don't stop to edit.

- Murder all doubt. Doubt is inevitable; in fact, it is built into the writing process. Ignore it. Bully it. Tell it to screw itself. You're the best person to write this piece who will ever exist because it comes from you. Act like you own it, because you do.

- Focus, focus, focus. If you lose focus, take a five-minute break (the time it takes to brew a cup of tea) and then force yourself back to the task.

- Stay put as long as possible. A writer's success is contingent on the ability to plant his or her butt in a chair and stay there.

These items all revolve around the theme of maintaining your focus on a single task. Among doctoral students there are two sets of letters that get appended to them at the end of their time. One is PhD, for Doctor of Philosophy in their discipline—mine was English, obviously—and it is official. The other is unofficial but no less well-known for that: ABD, for All But Dissertation. The distinction here is that one group successfully wrote a dissertation while the other did not. The reason for the distinction is not that one group is smarter or better suited for the academic life but rather about the ability, call it discipline or inertia or what you will, to force oneself to stay in one place and write when there is no external pressure, no assignment, no due date rushing up, no authority figure breathing down our neck. There is no way of predicting, at least that I ever found, who will succeed and who won't until all the coursework and the qualifying exams are finished and the time comes to work independently. Some people just fall apart when the familiar rhythm and pressure they have known all their academic lives suddenly slides away, while others, the lucky ones, find the solitude and freedom congenial. You probably won't ever find yourself needing to complete a dissertation, but learning the discipline of staying planted and completing a writing task is one of the keys to writing success. Again I say: **you can't revise a draft that doesn't exist**.

When you finish this blast and have a first draft in hand, you're going to feel really great. Then you will look at this gem you've brought forth and it will look really . . . ugly. Continue feeling great; that's what it is supposed to look like. Embrace it. And, after a suitable cooling-off period to allow the elation to subside, get to work. But that is for another chapter.

What is needed here is a cautionary tale. There's a famous,

semi-apocryphal story about Jack Kerouac writing *On the Road* on a giant scroll of teletype or tracing paper sheets taped together and then publishing it.

Wait a minute! How can something be "semi-apocryphal"? It either is apocryphal or it isn't, right?

The "semi" gets appended because there is some element of truth here. There is a scroll, some 120 feet long, that Kerouac typed out in three weeks in April 1951. And the novel was published—in 1957. The before and after of the scroll, however, don't match the myth. Kerouac had taken multiple runs at telling the story starting at least in 1948, but none of them turned out as he wanted. He had yet to transition from the traditional narrative of his first novel to the fluid, jazzlike prose that would characterize his mature work. So then he decided to try this new form, taped a whole lot of paper end to end, and set sail on the novel. In between the April day when he finished and the publication date six years later, numerous changes were made, adding material, cutting the more overt sexual references (because it was the repressed fifties, after all), and removing descriptions that didn't fit or that delayed the forward thrust of the narrative. Many of those last wound up in the next book, *Visions of Cody*. But here's the issue in terms of our topic: that scroll is not the first draft. Those earlier, futile stabs are his first, second, and maybe third drafts, however much or little was produced. **Discovering what doesn't work is part of finding what does.** Those earlier drafts allowed Kerouac to work out the general shape of the narrative so that what appeared on his legendary draft was more about finding the language to tell his story than about finding the story. Even then, enough work was done on the scroll version that it is a fair distance from final copy.

The moral here is that the famous stories trip us up because we take the wrong lessons from them. We think the *On the Road* story is about genius bursting out in a boundless stream of perfect words, that Kerouac was the very embodiment of his pal Allen Ginsberg's writing mantra, "First thought, best thought." The much less sexy lesson we should take is that repeated failure (those first efforts) and plenty of time spent chewing on an idea, a plot, a work of art will bring a writer to the point of much easier creation. A touch of genius never hurts, of course. There is also an environmental angle to my interpretation: I'm just trying to help us all use less Scotch tape.

13

The Problem with Process

I can't write five words but that I change seven.
—DOROTHY PARKER

So YOU WANT TO write better? How much time do you have? How about a year? Does a year work for you? If you head off for your nearest college campus, that is about what you'll find at the Harvard of (insert county name here). I called my own university the Harvard of Genesee County, a play on the main campus where they put yellow wings on football helmets and refer to themselves as the Harvard of the Midwest. One of the tasks that will face you is a minimum of a semester and probably an entire year of composition instruction. I promise that you will become a better writer if only through ceaseless practice and reliance on what is known far and wide as "the writing process" or "the workshop model" or, bringing the two together, "process-workshop" writing instruction. The nomenclature and practice will vary from program to program, but nearly everyone has been teaching out of the same composition playbook since the midseventies, when I first became aware of it. The reason for this uniformity is simple: it works. Results are tangible: by golly, a fully revised, edited, critiqued, revised, critiqued again, edited again, and published essay is actually better than the soggy, sloppy first draft. Who knew?

Well, if it works, what's so bad about it?

Not a thing in the world. Only time. The real question should be: How much of that do you have?

Composition courses for decades have fetishized writing "process," this magical exploration of how far a single piece of writing can be poked, prodded, bullied, and belabored. Draft after draft, revision after revision until, in theory, a perfected final draft appears. There are two problems: first, that such sustained attention and group oversight can squeeze the life out of an essay (or a short story or poem, as critics of creative writing programs have long asserted), and second, in many cases, that such classes produce three finished pieces of writing in a fifteen-week semester. Most students will wind up with three essays or letters or analyses or whatever sorts of writing are required of which they can be justifiably proud. A few will produce work that is afraid of its own shadow, those over-workshopped items that want to go hide in the corner. But all of this requires the luxury of time to produce a fairly small body of work.

Writing rarely works out that way in the real world. Or in the academy. As an undergraduate (I should note that I was as nearly as possible an all-humanities, all-the-time student, hence the high number), I would produce nine to fifteen papers averaging six pages in a ten-week term. Later, I taught in a very good process-workshop composition program, and my students would write three pieces in ten weeks, often the only papers required (not being humanities maniacs) in their courses. Oddly, not that much writing is demanded of packaging majors; odder still, there are packaging majors.

There are exceptions, even in English departments. At the opposite end of the process scale, one of my colleagues taught an introductory course in reading and writing about literature, and he assigned short writing assignments for nearly every class in addition to three or four more formal essays, on the theory that more writing practice is better. Those smaller written items were not workshopped, revised, or published, nor were they intended to be. I fall somewhere in the middle: process is important, but it can't become an end in itself. Writing is rewriting, as the composition maxim goes, but it is also invention, creativity, problem solving, and vision.

That time element is why successful escapees of composition sequences rarely practice what they have had preached at them once they exit the workshop door. They can't. In my literature courses, I assigned, on average, three analytical essays in a semester. I gave out the assignments and writing prompts to direct students' efforts two weeks before the essays were due. Any later and they began in a panic; any earlier, they lost the thread and had to be prompted all over again. Those two weeks were ten or eleven days more than most of them used. Sometimes I would ask straight out in class how many had already begun. The answers were beyond dispiriting. More often, I would simply offer vague reminders, and the amount of uncomfortable shifting in seats told me all I needed to know. Students, like everyone else, like their instructors, are always pressed for time, of which they do not inevitably make good use.

I have called this a writing book for the rest of us, by which I mean, those who don't have all day, metaphorically speaking, to get the job done. Another part of "the rest of us" would be teachers outside the process-industrial complex who, for a variety of reasons, feel compelled to teach their students to write better. Some of them are undertaking this improvement on their own; others are actually compelled by Writing Across the Curriculum programs to offer writing instruction within the confines of their own discipline. Just like the average person tasked with a writing project, WAC instructors lack the luxury of time to fidget endlessly with drafts and revisions, or to set aside large swaths of time normally given to subject matter study. Even literature professors sharing English department real estate with composition programs are wary of giving over too much class time to process writing instruction. And they often began their teaching career in comp programs! The best that most of us, learners or teachers of writing, can do is to take the bits and bobs of process writing and use them as time and inclination permit.

If you follow the whole process, from invention to drafting to revising to polishing—especially if you are fortunate enough to find sympathetic others to workshop your drafts—and if you master a few niceties of English usage, you will be able to turn out perfectly serviceable writing. I promise.

Not planning to take a college composition sequence? Going it alone? Not a problem. You can do everything a course will do except for two things: (a) benefit from a ready-made audience, and (b) enforce the discipline to stick with the process. As for the first, you may be able to find a writing group through your local library or bookstore or even community education classes. In any case, you do not absolutely have to find a group if that proves too onerous. And for the second, take up some form of self-flagellation. Since I am generally opposed to violence against the self or others, I recommend extreme discipline in the form of a chair. Place your keister in said chair *every single day* and keep it there for a specified period of time. That specification can be whatever you want, just as long as it is sufficient to get some writing done. Be it ever so comfortable, in five days you will wish you opted for the willow switch. In two weeks, you will almost accept it as inevitable. In a month, you'll be a writer, or at least a person capable of becoming one. And you will have logged enough seat time to have completed at least one process-driven piece of writing. Probably more, since each time you take a few days to allow drafts to marinate, you have an occasion to begin a new project.

What about the problem? Didn't you say there was a problem with process?

Alas, yes. The problem with process lies not in our stars but in ourselves. Or time. Or ourselves in time. There isn't enough time to go through the process in the prescribed fashion either because we don't start soon enough or because circumstances beyond our control dictate a much tighter timeline: "That report on the survey results is due tomorrow, Smithers." Of the two, our procrastination is by far the more likely, as I indicated earlier with the paper assignment anecdote. The long and the short of process issues is that we rarely wind up having time for the whole business. Done right, the process takes about three weeks, most of which is pausing for fermentation. Writing isn't all that different from making sauerkraut: it's messy and rather unpleasant, and there is a lot of waiting.

But we don't have time to make kraut. We barely have time to eat it; there's a deadline ahead! What are we to do?

Here's where having practiced the whole composition-class writing-process discipline comes in handy. Students have an advantage here. In college and even many high schools, there will be a cadre of people whose job it is to instill that discipline. You might apply a different word from "instill," but I have been one of them, and that is really what they are attempting. It is the best preparation you can get for your future writing endeavors. If you are not a student and not likely to become one, you can approximate the instruction (minus the group feedback and instructor comments on drafts) by following the procedures you have read about earlier on the writing process. But here is what every writing instructor knows: the moment the class ends, students are *never* going to employ the process the way they have been taught to do it. The only real hope is that they have absorbed enough of the lessons to fashion some abbreviated process that works for them. Imagining that these people with whom you have just spent many weeks inculcating productive habits are going to backslide to their pre-instruction routines is just too disheartening. So we tell ourselves that our students have learned enough to practice better writing habits than formerly, something I happen to believe they mostly do even if they deny it. They will at least think about the three or four or five stages of the process, and awareness leads to better outcomes.

It may sound as if I have just accused the human race of being lazy and slovenly, but that's not true. I have only suggested that it is human, that it is, approximately, like me. Who may be lazy and slovenly. Being only human, we need to streamline the process down to *a* process, *our* process, which will mean paring away some of the steps that an instructor would insist on. We will rarely undertake four or five invention activities. One or one and a half will have to do. At the other end, we may have to cut down from two edits to one, along with a revise-as-you-edit contraction, even if we know the best result will come from keeping these steps intact. In the real world, a lot of elision takes place in the stages of the writing process, not because we want it that way but because we can't manage it the right way. That's okay, though. If we practice *some* process and do so diligently (more or less, being human), we can learn to produce better essays, newsletters, opinion pieces, anecdotes, profiles, reports, or any other form of writing we need to produce. I have a relative who started his journalistic career writing obituaries of local notables for a small newspaper. This was once a fairly common starting task for new hires. With practice, you can even learn to produce lively writing about dead people. And if you can do that, you can do anything.

14

Detailing Your Prose (1)

Don't tell me the moon is shining; show me the glint of light on the broken glass.
—ANTON CHEKHOV

WRITING WITHOUT SPECIFICS IS just so much blather. You can have the best ideas, the best story, the best analysis, but without details, it's all just blah, blah, blah. And not just any details but what we have called since Anton Chekhov the *telling* detail; that is to say, the detail that brings things to life or moves the work forward in some significant way. "He opened the door" doesn't tell us much. "He opened the red door" isn't much better unless red is going to turn out to be a massive clue, which it could. "As he shouldered open the red door, it squeaked on its rusty hinges." Now we're getting somewhere. That one has visual, auditory, and even tactile information. That's a detail a writer can work with and, better still, a reader can sit up and notice. Whether or not it amounts to a telling detail, the writer will have to determine. Since I am the writer, I can state that for now it only exists in the realm of theory. The holy grail of telling details is the six-word story often attributed to Hemingway, "For Sale, Baby Shoes, Never Worn." Three details, each absolutely crucial to meaning. Most of us will never craft anything quite so perfect, but we can move closer to it with practice.

Where do we even begin on a subject as massive as detail? Maybe with the understanding that the need for specifics transcends genre. Fiction, certainly, but narrative of all sorts lives and dies on tangible items that readers can reach out and touch, grasp, turn over and examine, and use to understand the story being told. Readers have to see, hear, taste, feel the story as it unfolds; otherwise, it doesn't really exist. In his exquisite short story "Cathedral," the late Raymond Carver ends the story with the narrator, who begins the story by disliking and fearing the blind man (as the narrator insists on calling him), Robert, who has come to visit, helping Robert "see" a cathedral by guiding his hand over a sheet of paper as they draw one together. This act of hand touching hand demonstrates in a way that no amount of explaining ever could that the narrator has overcome his earlier aversion to this visitor so different from himself. The scene is also a near-perfect metaphor—except for the bigotry, which we will pass over—for the duty of the writer, who must help his readers envision not only the action but also its consequences in his story. He is forever assisting us in tracing cathedrals we can't see.

Details are no less essential for nonfiction narrative, but the supply is more limited: you don't get to make them to order. If you are writing a history of the Lewis and Clark expedition, you don't get to make up a fight with natives that never happened. That's okay, since the travails were abundant without that invention. In his *Undaunted Courage: Meriwether Lewis, Thomas Jef-*

ferson, and the Opening of the American West, Stephen Ambrose details an encounter between the men and a grizzly bear as recorded in Captain Lewis's journal in which the bear took a total of ten musket balls, half of them in its lungs, then swam halfway across the Missouri River to a sandbar where it took another twenty minutes to die. After they saw another grizzly a week later that swam away, Lewis noted rather tartly that "I find that the curiossity of our party is pretty well satisfyed with respect to this animal." Ambrose has the advantage of relying on the letters and journals of Lewis, himself an excellent writer notwithstanding orthography that drives my spellchecker to nervous collapse. Lewis supplies the telling details on which Ambrose relies, always handy for the modern writer looking at the past. Absent the accurate count of shots that reached their target without killing the great bear, readers can't really understand the danger that faced the Corps of Discovery. Even allowing for the relative ineffectiveness of flintlock muskets as compared with modern centerfire rifles, we understand that the grizzly was an incredibly tough beast.

The other thing that occurs here is that the encounter with the bear becomes a metaphor for the broader perils faced by the Lewis and Clark expedition. This new country they explored was vastly bigger, stranger, and more hazardous than anything in their existing frame of reference. There is a writing truism that one cannot convincingly represent the universal except through presentation of the local. In this case, there is no single sentence or paragraph Ambrose could write that would capture the different magnitude of the West compared with the world they knew. But in comparing the grizzly with the black bear the men knew from back east, readers can see the difference in scale as emblematic of the larger situation the Corps faced.

Poetry relies on the concrete and specific more than any other written form. A poem can consist of nothing but details:

The Red Wheelbarrow

so much depends
upon

a red wheel
barrow

glazed with rain
water

beside the white
chickens.

This gem is by modern American poet William Carlos Williams and uses the simple, local, and homely to make whatever point readers may take from it. Indeed, readers will often finish the poem and remember it as only being the last three stanzas, which make it an object poem. But the first two lines provide context for the sharply rendered images, causing us to ask: What depends upon them, and how does it depend, and why does it matter "so much"? Williams declines to tell us, only suggesting that something depends for some reason, which hints at the possibility that the answers lie not in the poem but in ourselves.

A few years ago I began writing what I call, after seventeenth-century philosopher Blaise Pascal, "Pensées," which means both "thoughts" and "pansies," like the summer flower. In his work and in mine, meaning is carried largely by the details from nature, ordinary and singular scenes of a magical world we notice too infrequently. Shying away from calling what I do "poetry," I usually refer to them as "verselike objects," although they sometimes come, as did this one, as prose poems.

Sudden Death

The strike comes as I cross the short bridge in a snow squall,
the Cooper's hawk snatching the cardinal in a scarlet
explosion. The windshield is a movie screen against which
the drama of living and dying plays out in a swirl of white
flakes and red feathers.

The images are just as they announced themselves in the moment, larger bird attacking smaller, then vanishing, leaving behind a handful of feathers and a slightly stunned observer. I felt the need to capture it as exactly as I could, leaving any conclusions (following Williams in my clumsy way) to the reader. The first draft, by the way, was nearly twice as long and laden with observations and musings that were not nearly as interesting as the event that occasioned them. The entire revision process, then, was one of paring away, getting as close to the bone as I could. I very much recommend, by the way, that you try this yourself—not going around looking for violence in nature but observing the world as you see it and then capturing it as accurately as you can. The results may surprise you. Details carry you a long way if you learn to trust them.

What, though, makes a detail "telling"? That's the question, isn't it? A detail is just a detail unless it connects in some special way to the story or poem or discussion at hand. At that point, the detail is just a piece of rubbish, best discarded. And don't even consider stacking up more of its kind; all that makes is a pile of rubbish. For the detail to become telling, it really does have to convey some significant message that won't be unlocked any other way. Consider the following: "While paddling my kayak, I developed a blister on my left hand. Soon, I knew, my right would follow suit." Yeah, so? That's what you thought as you read it, right? Now, try this version: "In the middle of my second hour of pulling upstream, I realized that I had fished too long, drifted too far, and left myself too much work to get back to the landing. The newly formed blister on my left hand drove home my folly with each stroke." In the first example, we see Sigmund Freud's point that sometimes a blister is just a blister. I'm pretty sure he said that, or should have. That is a random fact, announcing nothing but itself. In the second, that's a skin lesion we can work with, a self-accusation by the speaker manifesting as an injury. What we really need from detail is that first of all it be itself (nothing worse than a phony detail) but then encapsulate some essential element of the story that, being intangible, is not immediately graspable in readers' minds.

Brandi Reissenweber of the Gotham Writers Workshop says of the "telling detail" that it "captures the individuality and uniqueness—the very *essence*—of what is being described. It doesn't simply inspire an image in the imagination, it also sug-gest[s] an abstraction, such as meaning or emotion. And it does all of this with brevity." She goes on to offer a famous example from F. Scott Fitzgerald's *The Great Gatsby*: "There was music from my neighbor's house through the summer nights. In his blue gardens the men and girls came and went like moths among the whispering and the champagne and the stars." She goes on to comment on how the description begins with something factual, the music and the nights, then moves to the casual, flirtatious mood of these gatherings, the loosening of tongues and behaviors attendant on alcohol consumption (in the middle of Prohibition, as it turns out, although Fitzgerald couldn't know that), the general decadence, even working in the comparison of "flitting" moths to the immensity and permanence of the universe (the stars). The only thing I would add is that the moth simile emphasizes the insubstantiality and brevity of it all: these things and people may be bright and shiny, but they are flimsy and will vanish suddenly. Although the reader cannot know this so early in the novel, Nick Carraway, the narrator, most certainly does, telling the story as he is somewhere after the struggle and calamity to come. This is the sort of scene that floats back into our consciousness when we look back on the book precisely because it is so prescient without giving anything away too soon.

That is how telling details work. When they are well-chosen, they convey messages without requiring explanation. In fact, if you feel the need to explain, either you haven't presented it well or the example is not the right one.

If you want to see details used to great effect, look to the movies. Unlike written entertainments, film by definition can't fall back on abstraction and blather. Virtually every frame of a movie has specific visual information in it. Even a shot of an empty blue sky is of something tangible. Moreover, the trinity of screenwriter, director, and cinematographer spend their lives looking for images that will eliminate the need for something to be said in dialogue. Words are never as convincing in movies as images. This basic truth was demonstrated for the first three decades of moviemaking before synchronized sound was invented. When Charlie Chaplin's Little Tramp and his roommate Big Jim McKay (Mack Swain) are on the verge of starvation in *The Gold Rush*, Big Jim looks at the Tramp and he (and we) sees a giant chicken. Of course it's a gag, but it also tells us, without telling, what is happening in his brain. When a man disgusted with himself is sitting at a bar, there will be one of a host of polished surfaces, most commonly the mirror behind the bar or the shining surface of the bar itself, to give back to him the image he most loathes. Film is an excellent course in how to make images work for the storyteller and by extension for every writer.

"Another mantra, which I still write in chalk on the blackboard, is 'A Thousand Details Add Up to One Impression.' It's actually a quote from Cary Grant." That's from John McPhee's *Draft No. 4*, and it contains a beautiful example of what he means. In declaring that the quote is from Hollywood star Cary Grant, he tells us not only that he finds it apposite to the writing craft but that such reliance on detail carries over to other art forms. McPhee knows whereof he speaks, having written for *The New Yorker* magazine and published books for nearly sixty years at the time he wrote that passage. We need always to keep in mind the value of specifics in writing, in finding the great, the small, the telling details that will elevate our work from the mediocre to the sharp, the brilliant, even the sublime.

In case you're wondering, Hemingway never gave that example with the baby shoes, unless it had quotes around it. Not his, some other guy's, although which guy is contested. Which offers us another lesson: make sure to get your details right.

SOARING PRACTICE

15

Exercises from Literature

Imitation is not just the sincerest form of flattery—it's
the sincerest form of learning.
—GEORGE BERNARD SHAW

AT ONE TIME, COMPOSITION instruction comprised copying out pieces of established work: openings of novels, individual lyric poems, endings of short stories, whole essays. And in truth there is a lot to learn there, mostly about how someone else did something that you weren't planning to do. That model strikes us nowadays as too static. Better to begin with a dynamic exercise that moves toward developing the aspiring writer's skills. We could, for instance, tell her to write out William Carlos Williams's "This Is Just to Say":

> *I have eaten*
> *the plums*
> *that were in*
> *the icebox*

and which
you were probably
saving
for breakfast

Forgive me
they were delicious
so sweet
and so cold

Our student would learn something about how Williams composed this poem. If, on the other hand, she were to rework the poem into her own apology, following the form but choosing her own content, she would learn that prior lesson but also begin forging her own path. We can use earlier writing not merely as a model but as a springboard to something new. The possibilities are endless.

Yes, I said earlier that this is not a handbook on fiction or poetry or dramatic writing. Still true. On the other hand, that doesn't mean we can't learn techniques from them that we can apply to any writing activity we choose. Plus, you never know when you might, like me, find yourself writing your own *pensées* or verselike objects or something else you never imagined you would do until the mood strikes you one afternoon.

It has ever been my policy to filch from the best, and I'm too old to change now. Besides, this one is special: I'm pinching from the best an insight she stole from the best. Back in the middle of the twentieth century Joan Didion was part of a group—assuming we define "group" very loosely, since they agreed to no single program and paid no dues—of like-minded writers who revolutionized journalism. Their innovation was so radical that it acquired a name: *New Journalism*. As disparate as their approaches to this *new* thing were, what these writers—Tom Wolfe, Hunter S. Thompson, Norman Mailer, Gay Talese, and many others, including Didion—brought to the project was that they were fed up with the old journalism, with doing the same old stories in the same old ways. And they brought novelistic sensibilities and techniques to their novel approaches. It is hardly surprising that many of them either, like Didion, came from the world of fiction writing or would go on to produce noteworthy novels. What they did that differed from earlier journalism involved scene structure, use of language to set tone and mood, inventive narrative approaches (including something very like stream of consciousness), and heavy use of dialogue to reveal character and story. If this does not sound wondrous and strange to you, it is because you became a reader of nonfiction after they had worked their magic.

Among that august company, Didion stood out for three things. First, she was a woman and brought a sensibility distinct from the boisterous boys. Second, her true subject was California, or rather California as experienced by her or filtered through her consciousness. And third, she sounded more like Ernest Hemingway than Hemingway did. She perfected his short, clipped, perfect sentence so much that a word often attached not to her but to her sentences is "lapidary," meaning "cut and polished like a gem." And in "Last Words," an essay first published in 1998 but only collected in her 2021 *Let Me Tell You What I Mean*, she tells us that she was so taken with the opening paragraph, a mere 126 words, of the master's *A Farewell to Arms* that she "studied them closely enough and practiced hard enough [that] I might one day arrange 126 such words myself. Only one word has three sylla-bles. Twenty-two have two. The other 103 have one."

And did she ever. That's an exercise for the ages. In a sense, though, it is a very old practice. For centuries, pictorial art students learned from the masters by copying their works. Often the best of them went on to work as assistants in the great artists' studios. We occasionally still hear of them when a heretofore unknown painting attributed to, say, Rembrandt or Titian turns up, sparks imaginations among the collector class, and then resolves with a declaration that it was actually by his assistant X, who made a copy of the original, now lost. I have never subscribed to the belief that writing out, word for word, prose from great literary figures actually advances our own prose style. From a compositional standpoint, an individual word (like "word") looks the same from Hemingway and Faulkner and, well, me, allowing for variations in fonts, which have nothing to do with the writer in question. We learn nothing like brushwork from that word on the page. We are better off to work as Didion does in her essay, taking the passage apart, analyzing it, and seeing what makes it tick, not with the goal of repeating it but rather of repeating its lessons. There are writers who claim to have learned the secrets of the masters by copying out huge passages by Shakespeare or Hemingway or Toni Morrison, and they probably did learn a lot. I suspect, however, that since copying text requires attention but not a lot of thought, their minds almost automatically start taking things apart. Is that because of the copying or only because of seat time in front of a text? Not that it matters; if it works for you, go with it.

In Didion's case, what she learned from Hemingway was not mere brevity but elision; her art, like his, was the art of leaving things out. Hemingway has a story, "Hills Like White Elephants," in which a couple—the "man" somewhat older and more worldly and the "girl" not exactly a girl but a younger woman whom he seeks to manipulate—have a raging argument over something that is never named but that is clearly tearing them apart. They do everything except mention the procedure in question, and the longer they go the more frustrated they get. The word? "Abortion." And with it, "pregnancy," which is likewise avoided. Some few readers get to the end of the story (it is quite short) and have no idea of the source of so much strife. Usually, they are extremely literal-minded, vacuuming up everything that is said, but if something isn't expressed directly, it causes them problems. Hemingway forces us to watch the surface discussion and discern what lies beneath—the hidden part of his famous iceberg theory, by which he means that the visible part of a written work is only a tiny portion of the knowledge and vision that drives it, the way an iceberg's greatest mass is underwater and therefore hidden. So, too, with Didion. She takes us to the point of revelation and leaves us to see what remains unrevealed. When she describes a "recording session" by The Doors in which nothing is recorded or even rehearsed, in which front man Jim Morrison arrives unforgivably late, distracted or stoned, to the surprise or even irritation of no one in the studio, and which trails off into irresolution. Having shown all this, without overtly judging, she informs us that the record took "some weeks" to get finished and states, with Hemingway flatness, "I did not see it through." There are conclusions to be drawn, about the group, about youthful self-involvement, about fame, about many things, conclusions she has taken us to the brink of making but declines to state openly.

Here's what I say about using literature to learn to write

better: do what you have to do. If you see a three-word phrase you really like, abstract out the pattern from the actual words (adverb-adjective-noun, for instance) and write it with three other words of the right types. If the phrase involves alliteration (repetition of the first sound) or assonance (repetition of vowel sounds), do not fail to do so as well. That soundscape may be the key element.

🖉 The novelist John Gardner, whom we discuss elsewhere, would typically leave blanks in his sentences where he wanted a word with a certain rhythm. The rhythm he knew but the word momentarily eluded him. What he would put in the blank, if he wanted an anapest, a three-syllable word with the third syllable accented, would be something like "da-da-DA." At some later point, he would go back and find an anapestic word (or maybe two words with that combined meter) with the meaning he desired, and plug it into the gap. To be sure, Gardner was fussier about the rhythms of his sentences than most of us can afford to be, but the point is, you can learn to do anything. You may, for instance, want two accented syllables one after the other as a sort of punctuation and meaning "completely mistaken," and you can't come up with a phrase. Leave yourself a blank spot and a parenthetical note to that effect, and in revision you may just stumble across "DEAD WRONG." Capitals optional, of course.

🖉 Imagine for a moment that every character in a play believes that the action is really about them. Tom Stoppard used this possibility to turn *Hamlet*, which is about the eponymous prince, into *Rosencrantz and Guildenstern Are Dead* (1966), in which the two hapless courtiers spend most of their time sitting in the wings of that *other*, more famous play until their cue comes. Try it. You don't have to write an entire play or novel. Just think of a story that focuses on, say, Ophelia or Queen Gertrude instead of Hamlet. Sketch out how the story would play out, what we might learn (and what you would have to invent). Or take Henrik Ibsen's *A Doll's House* (1879), in which the "good" wife Nora chafes against the constraints of her suffocating marriage until in a shocking conclusion, she leaves her husband and children. What sort of story do we wind up with if instead of Nora we focus our attention on her husband, Torvald? Or the sympathetic but dying Dr. Rank? Or the blackmailer Krogstad? You can do this with any play or movie or novel or story you want. Someone is always left underdeveloped in a literary work. What will you learn? For one thing, that every story—fictional or real-world—presents options for how it might be handled. There are almost always ways to present any information other than the one that occurs to you first.

Bend It Like Beckham—these next three are a single unit. First, write a paragraph describing a scene: the view out your back door, a nearby park, an industrial park, a farm you pass while driving, anything you see that you can describe in some detail.

Second, rewrite the paragraph in the manner Ernest Hemingway would. You can find plenty of examples of Hem's prose even if you don't know it well. What you are aiming for is a flat description: short sentences, nouns and verbs, very few if any adjectives and adverbs, facts, not feelings.

- Third, pick any writer whose style you admire (or maybe despise) who is not Hemingway or a copycat. Write the paragraph in the manner of that stylist.

- Transcribe a conversation you have with someone. Include all of it. Then edit it to make it more effective. Do not invent new lines. Cut whatever needs to be trimmed. You may move lines around, but not if it changes the meaning. The point is, eighty or so percent of real-life conversation is slop. We're not very efficient speakers because we don't need to be and because efficiency is tiring. If we all spoke as if we were in an Elmore Leonard novel, we'd be exhausted all the time. Note: do not *ever* publish that conversation or your edits without the permission of the other person! Your best plan would be to learn from the exercise and burn the results.

- If you aspire to play shortstop professionally, you had better be prepared to field a lot of grounders in practice. Hours upon hours of practice. For years and years. Why would writing be any different? My late friend Jim Cash used to sit in the Michigan State Union every afternoon writing dialogues between "He" and "She." He would construct a situation that would provoke the two speakers to need to talk to one another and then turn them loose. He sometimes wrote one and then went back and wrote it again while throwing in a wrinkle, something that one of them said early that he or she hadn't said the first time, and then went at it again. And then again. The result? At his best, as in *Top Gun*, his dialogue sparks and crackles. You may not want to write in conversation-heavy genres, but whatever your chosen form is, there is only one way to get better. Same way as getting to Carnegie Hall in the old joke: practice.

- The late novelist John Gardner, who was a brilliant teacher of fiction writing, was something of a genius at creating these challenges. Here's an example: describe a building from the point of view of a man whose son has just been killed in a war, without mentioning the son, the war, or death. Once you have the principle, you can create a lifetime of exercises. In fact, he builds off that one by assigning a second description of the same building (I always see a barn in these, but whatever works for you) from the point of view of a happy lover, minus any mention of the loved one or love. These sorts of exercises are about controlling tone, mood, and release of information. Put another way, they are about evoking without explicit statement. And they are as useful for nonfiction writers as they are for fiction writers and poets.

- Plums and wheelbarrows. Go ahead, rework Williams's "This Is Just to Say" or "The Red Wheelbarrow" or any short poem that appeals to you. Change only the content words, keeping the structure and the function words so that the poem remains in form what it is in the original. Make it say something new.

Every writer needs to practice in order to correct weaknesses and to acquire new skills. This is something writing instructors do for their students: create situations wherein writers become better. We can do this on our own, however, if we are honest about strengths and weaknesses as well as diligent about working toward improvement. Not every person is good at this level of honesty about themselves, but we get better at it with practice. As we do, we become more adept at identifying areas that need more work for our writing to become better. Which makes us more confident and comfortable with the craft, which is always a good thing.

16

Writing Exercises That Illuminate Academic or Professional Tasks

Talent is cheaper than table salt. What separates the talented individual from the successful one is a lot of hard work.

—STEPHEN KING

A FEW MONTHS AGO, I heard from a ninth grader in California whose class had used *How to Read Literature Like a Professor: For Kids* about how the book had helped her, complete with a quote she found useful and a discussion of what she had learned, along with a question for me. How lovely, I thought, that she would bother to write to me about her writing experience. Then I got a second and third. Ah, I thought, this was an assignment. It still felt pretty good. I wrote back to those three, but the phenomenon was not finished. Over the next ten days, a total of sixteen came over the electronic transom. And they were all very nicely done. Then they stopped coming, and I assumed that was an end to it. It turned out it was only a lull over Thanksgiving weekend. The second wave hit, with greater numbers than the first, still adhering to the formula and carrying it out well. Just as I was about to write to the others from what was now phase one, I got buried with new obligations, so many that I had to resort to a sort of form letter with a set of responses to the various questions. Happily, there was a good deal of overlap in what the students wanted to know so the list didn't go to the full thirty-eight or forty. By now, a new thought had formed: I sure hope this isn't a county-wide assignment. I was beginning to have visions of the Dursleys and the torrent of letters coming down the chimney in the first Harry Potter movie.

But a somewhat nobler thought also presented itself: what a great assignment! And after all, I did not at all mind being the target of so much warm feeling. The prompt contained an audience (me), marks to hit, and a real-world purpose. Not only that, the assignment asked them to perform small tasks of literary analysis in identifying some significant aspect of the book and in interrogating the text—or at least the author—about some aspect. What more can one ask?

One of the problems of the American academic scene from elementary school onward has traditionally been the silo effect: we treat each subject, each discipline, each department as a separate entity, walled off from all the other entities within their own walls. This assignment asked students to reach beyond their expertise. Not every ninth grader aspires to study literature professionally. In fact, any number of them would find the idea somewhere between preposterous and horrifying. Quite properly, too. But in reaching out to a living author, they had to exercise a new skill. Whether they ever used it again was beside the point.

If I had my way, no student would graduate from a college-level program without some knowledge of a field that feels foreign to them. Or even that scares them. In part, this mania of mine is career related: humanities students—that is, those who study literature and languages, history, archaeology, anthropology, religion, philosophy, and the arts—frequently avoid the hard sciences and computational fields like mathematics and computer science. This avoidance becomes a lack of preparation for employment in today's market, especially at a time when the mythology is that humanities grads are "unemployable" or "limited" in their prospects. At the same time, the science types and computer jocks shy away from literature, the arts, and especially writing. Well, guess what, boys and girls. People who can write, and write like someone who understands the world, tend to prosper. Many engineers are shocked to find that a huge part of their work involves writing, the more so as they move up the corporate ladder. It may be true that English majors sometimes struggle, especially in tight economies, to find entry-level jobs, but a disproportionate number of them rise to become CEO of their companies.

Still, for better or worse—and I think we both know which—no one is about to make me the czar of American higher education.

Even so, we see examples all around us of fellow citizens who have prospered because they can communicate effectively. I know for a fact that it is possible to rise in the military from a second lieutenant counting enemy tanks to lieutenant colonel chiefly on the basis of being able to write reports, analyses, and, ultimately, speeches and position papers for superior officers. That LTC had been a student of mine. An officer who can really write, it turns out, is a military unicorn, quite rare and because of that quite valuable. Or consider Dr. Anthony Fauci, whose career took him from the AIDS crisis of the 1980s through the COVID-19 pandemic of 2020–22 not only because he had the courage to stand up to successive administrations but because he had the talent to convey difficult and sometimes abstract notions of immunology to government leaders and ordinary audiences alike.

Let's assume that we know the kind of informed, articulate person we wish to become or, if we teach, we wish to produce. What's the problem? I would say, chiefly, it is the lack of opportunities to learn to write better. Put another way, it is the ghettoization of writing. Think about it: Where does writing instruction happen? In writing classes. *First-year* writing classes. With catchy titles like "Composition One" and "Composition Two," a pair of things Dr. Seuss never envisioned but should have. Students generally enter these sequences with limited expectations of life-altering experiences, aside from possibly enabling them to improve their grades a notch or two on the rare paper assigned in other classes. Don't misunderstand: we absolutely need to bring entering students up to a certain standard—a minimum standard at worst—in their writing so that they have a chance of prospering in college.

But having taken that first useful step of staffing an English or writing department with capable instructors who believe in their mission, something they really try to do, universities then build walls around that very effort. The instruction in those composition programs is the last thing many students ever hear about improving their writing, including the possibility that they can improve it. If it were serious about turning out fluent writers, the American academy would insist on some combination of the following steps:

- A second or third writing class (because some programs require only one semester of first-year writing) placed during the junior or senior years.
- Regular instruction in writing in students' chosen disciplines in at least one or two required courses.
- Some sort of instruction late in students' careers that emphasizes the types of professional writing they may be called upon to perform.
- Regular assignments to write something useful—but well short of research papers—in the field. Consider, for instance, insisting that students in a course on the Civil War compose a press release for Lee's surrender. Or that students in a course on genetics write an explainer for the general public on the discovery of the DNA double helix.
- Ideally, every instructor in every course should embrace some small contribution to students' written literacy.

A swell idea, if I do say so myself.

Don't hold your breath. There are a host of reasons that there is rarely support for extending writing instruction out into the disciplines, and almost none of that resistance is nefarious. Adding another writing course would be expensive. There would be a number of new hires; maybe not new staff in each department but enough that university accountants would notice. In addition, some course, either an elective (loved by students) or a required course (loved by departments) would have to be cut for any new offering. It is not in the nature of universities to add, say, three credits and boost a round number like 120 to 123. Despite the sequence of digits, the latter is not a good look. Many faculty, moreover, feel unequal to the task of "teaching writing," as if it were an unlearnable skill. Mind you, those same faculty members (and I mean that from experience, the *exact same members*) have no problem with identifying their students' writing skills and diagnosing the shortcomings of the professional writing staff through whose courses those students moved. Some of their resistance is rooted in practical considerations: any class period given over to writing is a session not teaching content, and there are few enough of those as it is. Fourteen weeks and two class sessions per week of seventy-five to ninety minutes is never enough to cover everything a dedicated instructor wants to achieve. Now take out one of those twenty-eight; which part of cell structure are you willing to skip?

And finally, there is the matter of how many college instructors write very poorly. There is a reason this book is not called *How to Write Like a Professor*.

If you are an adult reader of this book, ask yourself how well you were prepared for your real-world writing needs in the course of your education. My guess is that your experience of writing in college, if you went that route, is much as I describe. In that sophomore-level writing course populated by seniors that I taught decades ago, more than a few soon-to-be graduates said the last essay they had to write in their college career before taking English 213 was in their first-year composition classes. And many said that was just how they liked it. Writing, after all, was a pain in the neck, full of uncertain outcomes and anxiety at every stage.

Everything I have asserted about writing instruction at the postsecondary level is also true at the secondary level. Finding time, finding energy, finding expertise to teach writing is nearly impossible for overburdened teachers at any level. The result is that, on average, most students graduate with just enough preparation to write at the minimum standard expected of that edu-cational level. *The minimum standard.* Is that the best we should hope for? We can do better.

This discussion is not a preamble to a recommendation to fix American education, although nearly everyone agrees that some sort of remedy is indicated. Besides, for a substantial number of readers of this book, that would come too late, your school days being in the rearview mirror. Whether your educational history is already recorded or surrounding you every day, our goal here is the same: we want to become masters of the written word. That takes work whether someone else assigns it or we undertake it on our own.

Teaching (or learning) writing in something other than composition classes is not hard to build in. Teaching an essay by Victorian philosopher John Stuart Mill? Have students write an op-ed using Mill as the source of information. It could be simply a learning exercise or a graded paper. And they should feel free to agree or disagree with the Mill passage in question. The other Victorians certainly did. The mere fact of death doesn't make him right. Or wrong.

What's that? You don't spend a lot of time teaching Utili-tarianism to tenth graders? That's no problem: use whatever is at hand. Source specifics don't matter greatly, only that the ap-prentice writers engage with the material in productive ways. Ta-Nehisi Coates, your local paper's editorial from yesterday, and *Doonesbury* can all be fair game. I'm less certain about *Beetle Bai-ley.* The goal is discovery, really: What do you think about this thing? What here lifts you up or irritates you? Pursue that. The grain of sand in the oyster creates the pearl.

This sort of exercise, for which I would suggest the name

quick essay, in the word's original sense of attempt or trial effort, is almost universally applicable irrespective of field. An article about the Federal Reserve, a chapter of a biography of Nefertiti, or a news story on a hypothesized new subatomic particle that may be a gateway to a fifth dimension (don't laugh, I read it just this morning)—all are equally valid occasions for a quick essay, a brief dive into a subject using one's instincts, prior knowledge, or reason as the means to break down this new intelligence.

The beauty of the quick essay is that it moves from knowledge of its source to ideas about it swiftly. That's why they are "quick." Just a hundred or so words, no research, and only ten or fifteen minutes. For best results, were I the instructor, I would comment on but not grade these trial pieces. This is an incisive learning exercise with the learning cutting in two directions: What does the material in question have to say, and what, why, and how do I think about it? Because we are answering those two questions, the act of grading detracts from the assignment's goals; suddenly, a third issue is introduced involving neither the writer nor the subject. Most of us can keep two objectives in view at once. Maybe that's because so much about us—hands, feet, elbows, eyes, ears—comes in pairs. Or maybe it is just that we possess limited intelligence and two variables are about all we can manage. Or maybe this assertion only applies to me and I am unfairly generalizing. Whatever the case, in my experience, concern about grades can interfere mightily with the learning process.

Nor would I necessarily comment on or even read every quick essay my students produced. Ideally, students should understand that these exercises exist for them as occasions for growth. We like, of course, to make sure our learners are on the right track, but that can be done with only occasional contact. Other ways to promote writers' growth are likely to produce greater benefit than a cascade of red ink. Producing lots of writing—or rather lots of *pieces* of writing—can move the needle for inexperienced writers in ways that working the same item over and over again can't. For one thing, everything we write has a beginning, middle, and end, and of those, the beginning can be the hardest: How do I start, what can I say to move the process forward, and how do I build on that first bit to create the second and third and so on? You may be thinking, but how will the writer know if she is on the right track if I don't tell her? Let go, Luke. Use the Force. Don't hold on so tightly. Most people will develop a sense of what works by trying again and again, with or without feedback. They will also discover, if no outside help is forthcoming, how to judge whether the thing they have made is good or not. Those of us who teach writing tend to overvalue our effect on those we help. All those great comments we make, all that sage advice! How can I withhold that from my students? If we are honest, though, we realize that most comments on work already done go unheeded and, in many cases, unread. I spilled enough ink on student papers to fill Lake Michigan before I finally admitted to myself that all that scribbling was a fool's errand. What it chiefly accomplished was to contribute to hand injuries. Mine, not theirs.

For that reason, the quick essay is an excellent exercise for nonstudents to undertake on their own. If you are improving your own writing, you can provide your own feedback: wait three days and read. I promise you, in the space of three days, you will be a different person from the one who wrote the quick essay in question. We will talk about revision later, but for now, just practice a wait-and-look approach to revisiting your work. The results will surprise you.

The quick essay is hardly the last word in writing projects that can be undertaken in classes or by writers on their own. Here are just a few among hundreds imaginable:

- Invent a news story—some big car pileup or person who survived a frightening ordeal or anything you can think of (if your imagination fails you, take some story from the actual news)—and write three different *ledes* for it. A lede, again, is the opening of a news account, sometimes spelled this way, sometimes "lead." You do not need to write the entire article. Each opening should begin with something radically different: time frame (for instance, one from just before, one during, one in the aftermath), viewpoint, perspective, whatever you want to change. Decide which one you prefer for the story you have imagined.

- Write a newsletter for a group or organization you might or do belong to. The collective does not have to actually exist. The events detailed can be realistic or fanciful.

- Take some bit of technical or scientific information you understand and write an explanation for readers who lack that understanding.

- Write a letter to a writer or artist or composer, living or deceased, expressing your thoughts on their work. The letter can be critical or laudatory; you might, for instance, wish to ask Claude Monet why his paintings are all out of focus or Winslow Homer why he has so many boats in his work. Your letter should be civil, respectful, and dignified while making its point.

- Write a letter to the editor (remember those?) expressing justifiable outrage at outrageous behavior some governmental body or individual has committed. Make sure your contempt comes across to readers while remaining civil.

- Write a letter to the editor about the same misbehavior while expressing no surface anger. How can you make your point without screaming it? Can you make readers see that point?

- Write a grant proposal for some ludicrous invention you wish to pursue. Make the proposal seem as sane as you can. Argue the case for funding in all seriousness.

- Write the first page of a report on behalf of the first landing party to arrive on Mars. Try it from two angles: first, on the day of arrival, and second, six months later when shelters have been constructed and life has found a routine.

What all of these exercises have in common is that they prompt the writer to consider perspective. How are these passages going to affect readers? How do they take into account the writer's greater knowledge? How does changing the point of attack alter the resulting account or change readerly expectations? How does leaving things out sharpen the focus? How does leaving things out make the article truer or less true?

Finally, there is a very practical bit of research every aspiring writer—which, by the way, includes those who don't so much aspire as know that they will have to undertake the task—should conduct: find a few samples of the kind of writing that you hope or perhaps fear lies before you, and tear them apart. Don't simply read them, although analysis always begins there. Once you know what each one says, discover everything about it. How does the piece introduce its subject and purpose? What sort of tone does it use? How long are the sentences, and how varied in structure? How much development is required? How does it deploy facts? Does it rely on sources, and if so, is the use obvious? Is the prose more formal than informal, or the reverse? How does the writer manage the ending? Until you can answer those questions, you won't begin to be able to absorb the form, much less produce it. Oh, it will be fun! You know you've always wanted to read a stock analysis.

17

Sentences and Their Friends

With sixty staring me in the face, I have developed
inflammation of the sentence structure and definite
hardening of the paragraphs.
—JAMES THURBER

QUICK, WHAT'S THE BASIC unit of meaning in film? Not that, it doesn't involve language. There were movies before there was synchronized sound. Remember that this is a visual medium and you'll soon have your answer: the shot. By "shot," we do not mean a static picture, although that can be a shot. But it can also mean an extended movement where camera or subject or both are in motion. As long as the same camera is focused on the subject (although the "subject" can be a vista that the sweeping camera takes in bit by bit), that is one shot. A long "tracking" shot in which the camera moves with the character as he walks along the sidewalk or runs from a bear is a shot. So is a static camera being approached by a moving speck on the horizon that slowly grows larger and larger until the speck has become a face that fills the screen. The point is, we can't have movies without shots, which are the units that add up to more extensive units, the scene (a collection of related shots that tell some portion of the story), the sequence (a related group of scenes that encompass a substantial storytelling arc), and the movie (which has a number of sequences arranged in a way that provides a complete narrative). Great edifices are built from small basic components.

So it is with written communication. Massive novels grow from single sentences. So do short stories, news articles, legal contracts, poems of almost any length, corporate annual reports, and letters to the editor, for however much longer we have letters. Or editors. Oh, sure, there are exceptions to the sentence thing, like that little stunt I just pulled with that fragment. In the main, however, writing in any language you care to name is composed of sentences. It therefore stands to reason that if we want to become better writers, composing good sentences is a skill we really should master.

Sentences are easy to learn, tougher to deploy: How long, how complex or simple, what words to use, how do we stack them in paragraphs? Often, the way we use language in writing is treated as a set of rules, a sort of plug-and-play linguistic machine. In reality, what we say and how we say it is largely governed by feel, which in turn is based on experience and expectations. What vocabulary choices are right for this audience? What tone am I trying to establish? Does *this* sentence accomplish *that* aim? And on and on. Again, the more writers understand that these decisions emanate from them and not from some arbitrary rules, the better and more fluent the work becomes.

Here is excellent news about you and sentences: you are an expert sentence maker and have known how to form them your whole life. Long before you could speak a complete sentence, you had absorbed the rhythm of sentences from your parents' speech. Before babies can articulate a single word, they babble in the sounds and rhythms of the language they hear. Which means that they are practicing sentences, with the rise and fall of sounds, in English or French or Vietnamese or whatever they hear spoken at home. In fact, infants who are taught sign language babble in—guess what?—sign language. Every story that was read to you and, later, every one you read yourself throughout your childhood reinforced the rhythms and word orders of your native tongue. And you began producing sentences when your vocabulary was still quite limited. "Me hurt" may not win any prizes in writing contests, but as a first effort, it warms a parent's heart. It also does something English sentences routinely do: putting the subject (even when the form of the pronoun is objective rather than nominative) before the verb. Soon you mastered not only the subject-verb sentence but the more advanced subject-verb-object. From there, it's all gravy. Not every language follows that word order; Latin called for the verb to pop up after the object (this is called S-O-V, or subject-object-verb order), often at the end of the sentence, which seems to English speakers a form of delayed gratification.

We arrive in adolescence, then, completely schooled in the basic English S-V-O sentence, and most will have added a couple of wrinkles: stringing two sentences together with a comma and conjunction to make a *compound sentence* or building a bit of hierarchy into the information string by making one part subordinate to the main clause (the part that can stand alone as a whole sentence) and thus creating a *complex sentence*. And you can tack on or slot in all manner of phrases and clauses along the way. The thing I never had to do in a college class was explain to students, to any student ever, what constituted a basic English sentence. How to make that form work for their writing? That was another story entirely.

Before we can discuss how to use sentences, we should establish what these things are. First, the unit itself: **a sentence is a statement that is complete in itself and can stand on its own without support.** That means that it has a noun (a person, place, thing, or abstraction—like an idea) and a verb (an action), often accompanied by an object or two (more nouns). Sorry, it can't be helped:

- He slept. (Subject pronoun + verb that doesn't require an object, called an *intransitive verb*)
- John hit the ball. (Subject noun + verb that does require an object—called *transitive*—+ object noun acting as the thing hit)
- Shannon gave her the book. (Subject noun + verb + noun acted upon + noun receiving the object. In this case, the indirect object [her] comes before the direct object [book]. English being what it is, the word order of direct and indirect objects can be squirrelly.)
- The ball was hit by me. (Passive construction in which the thing acted upon takes the subject position in the sentence. The other examples have been in what's called the *active voice*. Subject noun + passive verb form + preposition + object pronoun)

There, that wasn't so hard, was it? Okay, a little hard. Just remember that there are a mere handful of sentence forms: subject-verb (S-V), subject-verb-object (S-V-O), which can have direct and/or indirect objects involved, and passive construction (still S-V-O, but the relationship to the original action is backward, with the object moving forward to switch places with the true subject). In each case, there is an *actor*, an *action*, and usually a *thing acted upon*. Everything else is embellishment. For instance, take this passive sentence, "The suspect was seen by people." We can add specifics as to what he was seen doing, such as "leaving the scene of the crime," and numbers or other details about who did the seeing, but the structure remains unchanged: *"The suspect was seen* leaving the scene of the crime *by* several *people."* We could even add "green" to give a little color to those several people, which would render the sentence nonsensical, but the structure remains the same. But don't rely on length to identify simple sentences for you. You can add phrases, even longish ones, to a simple sentence and it remains a simple sentence. A preferred one is a participial phrase, meaning a phrase that begins with a verb form (usually ending in -ing) but lacking a noun in the subject position, as in this: "Hitting the ball hard, John drove in two runners." The phrase, lacking a subject, is helpless on its own and needs the main clause, which possesses both a subject and a verb. But wait, there's more. Depending on which information we wish to emphasize, we can switch which part is which: "John hit the ball hard, driving in two runs." As long as one clause is in charge, it's all good.

As you know, sentences don't all come in the same lengths. That is because they have different structures. The basic one, that beauty we have just examined, is the *simple sentence*, which is a single *independent clause* with no other clauses attached. Think of it as an S-V-O sentence with no additional S- or V- items.

If we take two independent clauses (those guys who can stand alone as sentences) and yoke them together with a conjunction like "and" **and a comma**, the result would be a *compound sentence*, which means that clauses have met as equals and formed a partnership: "John hit the ball, and two runners scored." I'm yelling at you here because to properly apply a yoke, **both** the conjunction and the comma are required; neither is strong enough to do the job alone.

So far, so good, but what if the partnership is unequal? What if only one of the clauses is independent? What if the other is merely a noun clause or a verb clause and lacks the additional words that would make it independent? Again, this being English, we merely attach new names and go forward. In this case, that second clause would be called a *subordinate (or dependent) clause* and the resulting sentence a *complex sentence*. Using our compound sentence example, we make one of the two partners subordinate to the other: "Because John hit the ball into the right-center field gap, two runners scored." The first, dependent clause has both a subject (John) and a verb (hit); it could stand alone, were it not for that pesky "Because." The grammatical term for such a word is "dependent marker word," meaning one of a set of words that can turn an otherwise independent clause into a dependent one by making the thought it expresses incomplete. In this instance, "John hit the ball into the right-center field gap" is a complete sentence on its own. Coupled with "two runners scored," another complete sentence, it requires more punctuation than a simple comma to connect them. Using the comma alone is called a *comma splice*. We could use a conjunction, "and," with the comma, but how many times do you want to use short compound sentences in a piece of writing? Try some variety. Live a little! The dependent/independent relationship can be reversed "John hit the ball into the right-center field gap, so that two runners scored." Okay, I admit it doesn't sound as good, but it is, if infelicitous, grammatically sound.

Are you sure we need to know all these terms and names? They're kind of a drag.

Kind of? They're a pain in the butt. A nuisance to learn and keep straight. If we hope to discuss our writing, however, we need a shared vocabulary in order to be mutually intelligible. Every field from auto repair to nuclear fusion has its specialized terminology, and writing is no exception. If you think this is bad, don't take up fly-fishing. To review: written communication is driven by sentences, which is to say by complete statements that form grammatical wholes. Those sentences can be simple, compound, or complex, which means that they can be arranged to emphasize relationships between the information they contain. They can also burst out in ways that these three categories utterly fail to describe. A "simple" sentence, for instance, can be tricked out with all sorts of modifying phrases attached in any number of spots in the main clause. An example? A moment ago, I said that a certain construction "is, if infelicitous, grammatically sound." I could just as easily have attached that modifying phrase "if infelicitous" at the end, after "sound." In fact, in first writing it, I did just that. No problem. English is one of the more flexible languages in terms of placement of words and phrases, which gives it that wonderful sinuousness and elasticity. The downside is that it also makes it hard to decide where to put which expression, especially for beginners. Hard-and-fast rules are so much easier. Freedom—learn to live with it.

So why do we care about these different forms? Because they

allow us to reveal hierarchies among our ideas. Simple sentences look orderly, but a profusion of them can be violently disorderly. Every simple sentence is its own organization; think of them as individual citizens secure in their identity and not inclined toward cooperation. "I'm me," they declare, "subject-verb-object and done. Now, leave me alone." There is nothing grammatically to cause them to make sense in moving from one to the next. Any semblance of organization, therefore, has to come at the semantic level, by what the words say and sometimes, as with Ernest Hemingway, what is not said. It is harder to be subtle in meaning while writing only simple sentences than it is with complex sentences because the meaning of each word is so critical to the movement of thought. At the other extreme is that complex sentence, which identifies at least one hierarchy by means of those *dependent marker words* that tell us: this next part is subservient to the master statement, the independent clause. Word meaning is still crucial, but now sentence structure is also sending messages about what matters more than what else, and that is accomplished with simple word addition. Appending "While," for instance, to the beginning of a sentence tells readers that, while the first part of the sentence will be important, it will be negated, overridden, or otherwise countermanded by the second part, which will be the dominant clause. We achieve this trick every day without even thinking, yet if we think about it just a little, we can do much more with it.

We have danced around this topic for a bit, appropriately, since the chapter is examining the role of sentences in the creation of a style. They are not, however, the entirety of style, so let's take a moment to consider fragments. We're all adults here. At one time, any discussion of sentence fragments in a book on writing would have consisted of a single word: don't. Their mere existence was an affront to good writing. They were not part of the creation of style but an indicator of its absence. Part of this predisposition against fragments was based on sound reasoning. First, a great many fragments that the writing instructor sees are the product of failed sentence recognition; the writer, through carelessness or inexperience, does not see that he has not produced an actual English sentence. Instead, what has occurred is either a noun clause or verb clause lacking the other key ingredient of independent clauses. As I often told my students, eighty percent or so of fragments are fixed by swapping a comma for a period, which will thereby attach the orphaned modifying phrase or clause to the main sentence to which it properly belongs. Poor little orphaned phrases! Not only are they frequently created by a lack of understanding (which writing teachers can't abide), but fragments can be and often are overused. They do not grow in power as they become more numerous. Quite the opposite, they are to writing what sage is to Thanksgiving dressing: a little adds piquancy, but in quantities large enough to notice, they become oppressive.

What our historical bias failed to note, however, is that, like sage, when used judiciously they add to the dish. A pinch here or there can accentuate or punctuate the prose. This may be especially true when used for comic effect, as with my "Poor little orphaned phrases" above, which undercuts my rhetoric before it can become too pleased with itself. They can be useful in conveying sarcasm or outrage or any number of sidebar kinds of points the writer wants to make. What they are not very good at is carrying the main argument, but we have complete sentences that are aces at that task. Nor are fragments invariably considered appropriate, particularly in very formal writing (think contracts and legal briefs, for example). There are, happily, many kinds of writing we wish to or are compelled to undertake, and not all wear tuxedos. So keep well-timed fragments in your writer's tool kit. Learn when and where they can be helpful and which parties they should not be allowed to crash, and you and they can accomplish great things together.

Pretty quickly, sentences demand to be put in some sort of order, grouped together like with like and arranged for maximum impact. In other words, we find that we need paragraphs. A paragraph seems like a product of rules and restrictions when we're being taught to assemble them, but they're really just sentences coming together to achieve a common goal. Think about what drives that need. It would be *possible* to shake out all the sentences that compose an essay or letter or lab report as one shakes out jigsaw pieces, with the understanding that the reader will assemble them into a pleasing order. But being possible and being acceptable are not synonymous. Readers would not congratulate you on your brilliant strategy. On their own, sentences are agnostic, neither believing nor disbelieving in a larger meaning. Each one means what it says, nothing more or less. Only when joined together intelligently do they open up further possibilities. A sentence does not seek out like-minded neighbors to organize into larger units; it is human minds, the writer's and, later, the reader's, that insist on order and meaning. We are the ones who organize sentences on a topic into larger units that can carry an argument or a narrative or a report or a letter forward to achieve some significant utterance.

We have talked and will talk again on how to arrange paragraphs. For the moment, let it suffice to say that a paragraph groups itself around a specific idea or event smaller than the work as a whole but certainly a part of it. To that end, writers typically set readers' expectations for the paragraph by identifying that specific thing around which the paragraph is built. As such, they are part of writers' ceaseless effort to move from chaos to order. If you have been writing for very long at all, you will have had the experience of cutting an otherwise good sentence out of a paragraph because somehow or other, it just doesn't fit. Sometimes, we may not be able to articulate how or why it rings false, but we feel that it does. It may fit better elsewhere, or it may not find a home anywhere. That will depend on whether it can advance some other paragraph's cause.

Most prose you will read (and likely write) will employ, for reasons good and sound, a variety of lengths and structures. As in much of life, too much of anything tends to cloy. Ice cream is a delight, but a diet of nothing but ice cream would lose its allure in short order, despite what some people claim. Short, simple sentences perform great work in speech and writing, but work that contains no other sort of sentences can easily wind up sounding like it was written by a child or a machine. And a steady diet of long, complex sentences simply wears readers out. There is another reason to mix things up stylistically: eventually, you are going to want to deliver a punch. And on this point, all sentences are not created equal. The punchiest sentences going are very short, hardly sentences at all. In fact, sometimes they may not be whole sentences but mere fragments. At the very end of *The Sun Also Rises*, Hemingway has his frustrated lovers, Jake Barnes and Brett Ashley, riding in a taxi. Their frustration arises from Jake's war wound, which makes sexual satisfaction impossible for either party. In her final statement, Brett blurts out, "Oh, Jake . . .

we could have had such a damned good time together." Jake offers a devastating agreement: 'Yes,' I said. 'Isn't it pretty to think so?'" That sentence contains worlds. Will Brett be able to hear the irony? Or the way that her claim ignores how good they have become at making a mess of their lives? Or how the assumption rests on fantasy yet might be true? In other words, it is perfect. It is hard for long, involved sentences to land that sort of worlds-containing perfection.

With one exception.

I saved this one for last because, well, you'll see. Before we leave this undoubtedly fascinating topic, there is one last sentence: the *periodic*. We have discussed at length the basic structure of the English sentence: subject-verb[-object]. There may or may not be an object of the verb, but if there is, it will follow the verb, which will follow the subject. But what happens if we upend that order, break expectations, and put something else last, maybe the verb? After all, not every language has the same reliance on word order. Some, like Latin, routinely put the verb at the end. In fact, early Latin, I am told (I wasn't there) used the verb-last construction with such regularity that there was no need for periods to signal the end. And that is what the periodic sentence is: an English sentence that is put together as if it were Latin. Used sparingly, it can pack a wallop. As with many things, overused, the structure quickly becomes mannered and silly. But here is what it can do. At the end of Henry James's novella *The Turn of the Screw*, the governess finishes her harrowing tale about two innocents in her charge and the malevolent ghost who has been pursuing them. She has been tightly squeezing the boy, Miles, protecting him (so she says) from possession by Peter Quint, the ghost in question. Miles answers her repeated question about what or whom he saw, saying, "Peter Quint—you devil!" But does the child mean that Quint was a devil or that the governess is? We never know, because this sentence comes next: "We were alone with the quiet day, and his little heart, dispossessed, had stopped." Those are the last words of the novella. Now that's a sentence.

Interlude

Rules to Live, or at Least Write, By

Do YOU KNOW WHAT the greatest threat to good writing is? The desire to be finished. And the greatest boon to good writing? Same thing. We all want to be done with tasks, whether it's cleaning out a stable (oh, man, do we want that one finished) or writing our novel. That last one could be disputed in the case of Leo Tolstoy and a couple of others one could name, but I think even Count Leo wanted to end both war and peace at a certain point. The thing is, tasks are processes, which are inherently unstable, and we are evolutionarily built to seek stability. So, we work hard and steadily. Or we rush and cut corners. We mistake first drafts for final, skim or skip over editing, fail to check our facts and sources. In other words, our haste makes us sloppy. The consequences can be grave.

Don't do that! In writing, haste really does make waste. Since this is a book on writing in English, of course I'm bringing in a bit of Latin, *Festina lente*, meaning "Make haste slowly." Translated from a Greek original, it became the motto for Emperors Augustus and Titus as well as for the much later House of Medici, among other notables. *Festina* is the imperative singular form (the verb mood you use to boss someone else around) of the infinitive *festinare*, which means, approximately, "Hey, hurry up!" *Lente* is simply "slowly." The phrase is an oxymoron, self-contradictory on the surface yet meaningful, but it proves so attractive that it pops up through the ages. Legendary UCLA basketball coach John Wooden adapted the concept twice, as "Be quick, but don't hurry" and "Never hurry when it matters." His championship teams were lightning-quick but almost never rushed. No need to be when you are nearly always ahead on the scoreboard.

How does this apply to writing? We might adapt it as "Work swiftly, but with all due deliberation." Not as pithy as "Hurry slowly," but it fits the circumstance. Accomplish those tasks where speed is appropriate with whatever quickness you can manage. For instance, write drafts in a burst if you can. Work steadily enough that you don't lose the thread of your piece. Once that is accomplished, though, slow down and be thorough in all aspects of your draft-improvement phase. Challenge every claim you make. Be sure that they are accurate, supported by facts, and backed up by solid explanations. Examine each sentence to make sure that it is (a) well-stated, (b) accurate, (c) in its right place relative to its neighbors, and (d) advancing your cause. Edit on the macro (ideas, structure, and general thrust) as well as the micro (the individual word-and-phrase level). We sometimes get so caught up in whether we have the right words spelled the right ways that we lose sight of the overall shape of the piece. Make sure that the overall design works, that it is clear and coherent, that it begins, develops, and ends well. In other words, pay attention to every aspect of your writing, which you cannot do if you are hurried or harried.

This idea is but one notion of the rules of the road for writers. Here are a few more things to keep in mind as you pursue the way of the writer. The good news is that there will be no parallel parking test. The road test? Every time you sit down to write:

1. **Write every day.** Inspiration is a mysterious thing, but I'm pretty sure it responds to your butt making contact with your desk chair. Pick a time frame that works for you and keep that appointment faithfully.

2. **Break Rule 1 as necessary, and don't beat yourself up over it.** Sometimes life intervenes. Sometimes you just aren't feeling it and need a day off. Sometimes you need to go fishing. I've had some good ideas on the river. Just don't let not writing become the default mode.

3. **Read. Widely.** Good writers are energetic readers. While you're at it, pay attention. You just might learn something.

4. **Know thyself.** You knew this was coming. If it was good enough for the Oracle at Delphi, it's good enough for me. Don't lose sight of who you are as a writer. Give yourself a chance to succeed.

5. **Remember your readers.** Who is it you're trying to reach? How best can you accomplish that goal? Keep them engaged from the first sentence to the last. Never let them go.

6. **Be clear.** There will be times when the subject or its treatment may lead to confusion. Don't let your prose be one of the sources.

7. **Any writing from a paragraph to a magnum opus needs a beginning, middle, and ending.** Make sure each phase of your work is doing its job.

8. **Obey the rules of good writing when you can; break them when you must.** Those things we call "rules" are

really averages of what strong writers do, based on observation. No one brought any tablets down from the mountain.

9. **Use your best words available in the best order**: active verbs, solid nouns, apt modifiers, the right word in the right place and not its second cousin once removed. The best words for you are those you would use in real life, not those you found in a vocabulary exercise. Sound like yourself, not a thesaurus.

10. **When in doubt, choose the simplest word that completely explains the situation.** This does not mean always use simple words. If a bigger word expresses your meaning more exactly than a short one, then that biggie is the simplest word that precisely conveys what you intend. I recently had occasion to use "demonym," which is the term used for persons from a given country or region, as in, "The demonym for a resident of Saint Christopher (colloquially known as 'Saint Kitts') is "'Kittitian.'" No kidding about either the place or the term.

11. **Write the best you can in the time you have.** Let this be your goal: if you meet your reader at some point in the future, he or she will thank you for what you wrote.

12. **Finish the job.** Do not stop writing until you have said everything that needs saying in the space allotted. Do not write one additional word. You want to leave your readers feeling, "I could read that all day," not, "I feel like I was reading it all day."

18

Oh, Yeah? Prove It!

*To believe without evidence and demonstration is an act
of folly and ignorance.*

—SOCRATES

OKAY, LET'S PRETEND YOU'RE a lawyer arguing a case in court. Yes, I know you're much too smart to go into the law, but humor me. You can be whichever side you want. Prosecutor? Fine by me. If you'd rather be Perry Mason, that works, too. First of all, you are on the side of right. If you're the prosecutor, the defendant is guilty as all get-out. If you're defending, your client is clearly innocent. You've got your approach down perfectly. You present your case brilliantly, and your closing argument is one for the textbooks. When the jury comes back, you lose. You either let a criminal walk or got your client sent to the hoosegow. What happened?

You didn't present any evidence. It was all rhetoric and over-confidence. Who let you be a lawyer, anyway? No prosecutor in history ever won a conviction nor did any defense attorney get a client off without producing evidence and countering that of the other side. No matter how persuasive you are, you have to come through with the goods. Otherwise, no sale.

Same thing with writing. Think of every piece of writing as an argument. That argument may only be, "Pay attention to me," but you're still trying to demonstrate that you are worth listening to. In that sense, a writer is like an attorney arguing a case in court. The good news for writers is that if they fail to adduce evidence in support of their argument, no one goes to prison. The bad news? No one is likely to be swayed by their writing. Every claim in a piece of nonfiction needs to be supported by some sort of evidence—facts, quotes, testimony, data—and the wilder the assertion, the more and better evidence required to support it. Not only that, the evidence needs to be pinned to the claim by some sort of logical connection, which means the writer is not off the hook just because a fact was cited. Even with narrative nonfiction, writers can't just deal in broad accounts. They must get down to specific events. In other words, evidence. Don't just tell us your hero had a tough childhood; show us his father, new stepmother, and siblings driving away from his home and leaving him to fend for himself in the woods at age twelve. That's what Daniel James Brown does in his masterful account of the 1936 University of Washington rowing team that won the Olympics, *The Boys in the Boat*.

In my research, I learned that there are four types of evidence. Unless there are five, seven, eight. Although there could be more:

- First, consider *facts*. The thing about facts is that they are objectively true irrespective of how one feels about them. Fact: Barack Obama was the forty-fourth president of the

United States, holding office from January 2009 to January 2017. You may admire President Obama or loathe him, but he was in fact president during that period of history. Gold, the element, has an atomic number of 79, meaning its nucleus holds exactly seventy-nine protons. If you find an atom of an element with seventy-eight or eighty (or any other number) of protons, it is not gold. Gold does not care about what you feel about it or about protons more generally. Facts are facts. They are objectively verifiable without manipulation. This is not to say they are not contentious. Facts are subject to interpretation, to being seen in different contexts, which is part of what makes life interesting. But only fools and knaves deny facts themselves. When news accounts reported in 2017 that President Donald Trump's inauguration had been more sparsely attended than President Obama's four and eight years earlier, the Trump public relations team pushed back, claiming that media photographs of the National Mall had been altered and producing a photo of their own that "proved" he had an overwhelmingly large crowd and not the half-filled Mall shown on television and in newspapers. Except that their photo was of Obama's 2013 inauguration, as both evidence of previous publication and metadata demonstrated. When exposed as having presented fraudulent evidence, they fell back on campaign manager Kellyanne Conway's phrase, "alternative facts." There were no alternative facts in this instance, only a sad attempt to deny reality with phony evidence. In this case, as in most, actual, not alternative, facts carried the day. Or maybe the day before.

Data are a form of facts involving numbers. "Data" is plural, but "datum," the singular form, is almost impossible to say in modern English with a straight face, so we often treat "data" as both singular and plural. Census numbers are a form of data, as are rises and falls in stock market indices. Those examples represent solid data, but there is also squishy data, such as public opinion poll results. In that case, the numbers are solid, but the basis for those numbers is subject to how sample respondents are selected, how questions are framed, and forty-eleven other factors. Squishier than that you cannot get. When you use data, you need to keep in mind that some is more reliable than the rest. Unlike facts (according to the accepted meaning of the term), data can and often has been fudged. We will talk more about evaluating data in the chapter on sources, but for now, just know that there are reasons to not accept everything at face value, as well as that it is incumbent on writers to do their best to use numbers responsibly.

Testimony comes in multiple forms, two of which are *witness* testimony—from someone who directly observed the situation in question—and *participant* testimony—from someone who actually took an active part, willingly or not. Both can be very useful as proof, to a point. People who witnessed or experienced a terrible event can be powerful voices, having had, as it were, a front-row seat. On the other hand, they can also sometimes be so traumatized that their testimony can be confused. There is a classic psychological study (that could never be done today) demonstrating that when an intruder runs into a classroom and does . . . something, no two people could give matching accounts of the action. It can be very difficult in some circumstances to see things clearly when the event itself is swirling and confused. I have been in a couple of close calls involving cars and ice. I have never had such clarity and focus as during those events; I have few memories more jumbled than what I recalled a short while later.

"Authoritative accounts" is a fancy way of saying "expert testimony." Scientists involved in an experiment are excellent sources of information, as are professionals who have dedicated their careers to studying any aspect of our world. It is fashionable in some quarters to discount the idea of expertise, particularly when that expertise contradicts falsehoods and conspiracy theories someone has "researched" online. Such claims against "experts" or "elites" (which seems to mean people who actually know things) usually arise from corrupt desires: someone wishes to sow confusion or discredit authoritative sources by putting out claims that run counter to facts. The goal is to produce such chaos that some target audience (dedicated followers, undecided persons) will be swayed by phony claims and spurious arguments. This strategy is known as *disinformation*, the deliberate spread of misinformation, although former Breitbart News executive chairman Steve Bannon more colorfully called it "flooding the zone with s**t." Breitbart's overall strategy was to produce countering, untrue assertions on virtually any subject, nearly all of it conforming to Bannon's fecal metaphor. Reasonable people, who seem

to constitute a slight majority, understand that denigrating expertise is an expression of malice rather than the pursuit of truth, and still trust authorities in pretty much all fields. As a writer seeking support for your claims, your best bet is always to cite experts.

Anecdotes (if true) and other stories can be compelling evidence in support of your efforts. In the case of narrative nonfiction, the specifics of stories make or break the narrative, bringing specifics and color to the larger tapestry. In arguments, they can bring life to what might otherwise be a bland or serious discussion. Throughout this book I use anecdotes and examples from my own writing or my interaction with student writers as a way of animating what is always threatening to become a dreary exercise. Nor do I do so without strong precursors. The great religious figures and movements use anecdotes, called *parables* in that context, to explain or reveal moral truths. Many of the best-known statements by Jesus and the Buddha are parables, and nearly every religion is built around a number of illustrative stories.

Quotes, paraphrases, and *general distillations* from oral testimony or written documents will show up in any sort of writing. Why use one over the others? Context. Direct quotations carry the power of being the actual words of a writer or speaker, which sometimes matters. If you are discussing the opening of the Gettysburg Address, a paraphrase just won't do. Readers expect to see the words Lincoln spoke that day, from "Four score and seven years ago" forward. "When Lincoln said that eighty-seven years had passed since the country's founding" is just not going to cut it. When the great man hands you solid-gold phrasing, use it. On the other hand, speakers can sometimes take a while getting to the point. That's the time for paraphrasing, for cutting down a large number of words to many fewer while retaining the meaning of the original. In more extreme circumstances, you may need to distill multiple pages of argument, say, down to their essence. To do so, you will care less about adhering to the immediate sense than if you were paraphrasing, but you will boil down those pages to a couple of lines. All of these approaches are permitted as long as in doing so you don't violate the original speaker's or writer's intent. To quote a writer but leave out the word "not" would be monstrous, but it is no less wrong to do so if paraphrasing or distilling. Omitting words is fine, unless the omission changes the meaning. Then, it becomes intellectually criminal.

This small catalog of types of evidence is hardly exhaustive, but it gives an idea of the ways you can support your writing, whatever it is. You recall that early on I suggested that your duty to readers is to grab them by the lapels and don't let go until you are finished. Since you can't achieve that state by force, you must do it by being interesting, and few things are more interesting than well-chosen evidence.

Choosing not only which evidence but which *type* of evidence is appropriate is an art in itself. Sometimes the choice is obvious. If you are claiming that most Americans support one of two choices—say, that blue skies are preferable to gray—there has never been an anecdote that can prove your assertion or its opposite. This is clearly the place for data, specifically public opinion poll results. If you can't come up with a respected poll that shows more than fifty percent support for "blue skies," you need to abandon the claim. You also need to look harder because, seriously, gray? Other situations will be less clear-cut. There are many instances where, for instance, either direct testimony or an anecdote could carry the day. Nor are these mutually exclusive; many times you'll see a piece of journalism with a supporting fact or data point and testimony from a witness or participant or expert or even uninformed person-on-the-street. The combinations are nearly endless and limited only by what the writer can cause to make sense.

Hey, don't stop! You're not done here. Choosing appropriate evidence is only part of the job; from there, it needs to be hand-fitted to the immediate task. Now that you've made your assertion and brought out your supporting evidence, there is another crucial chore. In fact, if you skip this step, you haven't accomplished anything. You have to pin the evidence to the assertion. If you cast your mind back to our discussion of the Toulmin method of argument, this is the *warrant* phase. Whatever you say in your anchor statement will be the *claim* that you have made. That will be followed by your *grounds*, the facts that buttress your claim. As we discussed, however, readers have a limitless capacity for misunderstanding, for disputing what you think is obvious, and for generally not getting with the program. The warrant, that sentence that wraps up the paragraph or the paragraph that wraps up the chapter, has one critical function: to take away from readers the wiggle room that will allow them to miss your point. Here, you say, is the clause in the Constitution or the law of physics (or perhaps something a bit less dramatic) that means that the grounds I have adduced make my claim valid.

At any point in this process, be prepared to rewrite some part you had thought was done. Let's say that, having decided on the evidence you use, you discover that it doesn't quite fit your anchor statement. You have three choices: look for different evidence, add another piece of evidence, or adjust your anchor statement so the two play nice together henceforth. If you know without question that your anchor statement is correct—not want it to be correct but absolutely know—then you chose the wrong evidence, or at least evidence that on its own is wrong for this spot in your work. If so, get different evidence or an additional item that modifies the first so that it fits the idea flow better. If the evidence is solid, you need to fix whatever is shaky in your anchor statement and elaboration. Bottom line: your argument and your evidence not only need to each be solid, they have to be solid *together*. Whatever stands in the way of that solidity needs to go. Right here is where your natural ruthlessness comes into play.

Whatever form your writing takes, readers want to see you follow through. If you make a claim, no matter how large or small, develop that, support it, and tie everything together. If you are writing a narrative and you say the abandoned boy was lonely, show us. How did he spend those first nights? How did he live on his own? How did he finally connect with other people again? Writers are always trying to convince readers of something, and the best way of accomplishing that is to show vivid and convincing evidence. If it makes the writer sit up and take notice, it will work for readers, too.

19

Even the Nile Has a Source

"Google" is not a synonym for "research."
—DAN BROWN, *THE LOST SYMBOL*

SEE IF YOU KNOW this one. In my life as a writer, I have occasionally found myself stuck fast in the middle of an argument, sometimes in the middle of a sentence, and once or twice in the middle of a word because I don't have the requisite fact at hand. Usually, I can just make a note to look something up, but once in a while the need seems so immediate that I have to go find out if, for instance, the line break in that poem was before or after the word "beside." I mean, who could bear such uncertainty?

At various times, we all need help with details, historical contexts, and plain old facts. That means we need sources. Nowadays, the mechanics of citing sources are covered by a number of online repositories such as Purdue's wonderful OWL (for Online Writing Lab) that can tell users how to meet the requirements for a number of major style manuals. The trickier part is using sources to convey your meaning. Here, rules don't help so much, except for this one: figure out what you have to offer and what your reader needs from you. Know those two things and you'll rarely go astray.

In my teaching career, I encountered every possible way of using (and misusing) sources including one or two I would have thought impossible. Some students almost never employed any information specific enough to require citations. Others plastered their texts with superscript numbers or, later on, parenthetical page references. In a seminar when I was a graduate student and in which we met at the end of the term to share our final papers, a classmate had fourteen citations in the first three pages. That's fourteen times turning to the last sheet to discover nothing more than a page number. The full paper had somewhere around forty-five in twelve pages. It was here that I learned that being overly scrupulous in matters of citation can be a disservice to readers, since many of her references were to facts not only in her same paragraph but from the same source paragraph and could easily—and safely—enough have been combined into single citations. She confessed to being terrified of inadvertently being guilty of plagiarism, which is better than being wholly unconcerned, but only a little for the hapless reader.

Writers absolutely must credit their sources, but the form that credit takes differs in academic papers, about which we have been thinking, and general-interest writing. In the latter, the need is as great, but the form is more relaxed. Most general readers are untroubled by which page carried certain information or the place of publication of the source. Simply mentioning the author and the article (with publication name) suffices in most instances. If you say that Malcolm Gladwell makes a certain claim in his book *Blink*, that's all readers—including this one—need. That said, it is important to know which sort of writing you are undertaking and what the rules for citation are.

Most of the major style manuals switched during my career from demanding endnotes or footnotes to using a Works Cited page and simply placing the author's surname and page reference in parentheses following the borrowed information. This change was a boon to humanity, since turning to the back of a paper simply to find a page reference was a nuisance, while having to leave space in a typed paper for footnotes at the bottom of the page was a nightmare in the manual typewriter days. I remember discovering this change with not a little envy on behalf of my earlier self: "If only we'd had this system back then . . ." Notes, either of the foot- or end- variety, are limited these days to what are called "content notes," sidebar information or arguments that don't fit neatly in the context of the wider paper or chapter but need saying for one reason or another. Content notes are often the most entertaining portions of scholarly papers, particularly those written during an academic feud (of which there are many).

In *Merchants of Doubt* (2010), Naomi Oreskes and Erik M. Conway demonstrate how, beginning in the 1950s, a group of highly educated, malign influencers (as we would now call them) managed a series of disinformation campaigns to mislead the public on matters beginning with the smoking-cancer link and moving on to climate change and assorted other hot-button topics. They did so by publishing papers that contained questionable or outright false information and then ceaselessly citing one another until eventually it was impossible for average persons to find their way back to the original lies. (*Disinformation* is the deliberate, often coordinated act of spreading *misinformation*.) The first-generation deceivers were rabid anti-Communist right-wingers, but their template has been emulated by bad actors of every nationality and political stripe. That book is hugely important, but it raises a critical issue for writers: If it took sixty years and two academics to unmask this unholy alliance of anti-Communism and Big Business to produce junk science, what hope is there for a student writer or a nonprofessional researcher to judge sources? Indeed, it can seem hopeless to try to separate wholesome information from toxic attempts to mislead, but there are some things we can do.

The first is to examine credentials. Just what justifies this person writing as an expert on this topic? And what we need to understand is that credentials rarely extend beyond the holder's narrow field. I have a PhD in English. Sounds like I know things, doesn't it? I do, within limits. My specialty is English and American literature from about 1890 forward. When it comes to literature from other countries or from earlier than that date, my knowledge is spotty—more than nonscholars, but only by a little. I have been reminded of this by a conversation I have recently been having with a Shakespeare scholar, compared with whom I am a rank amateur. Outside the field of literature, I'm hopeless. The physical sciences are interesting but only from a distance. I know enough medical terminology to talk to doctors about my health, but I learned most of it the hard way. In any event, you don't want to take my word for anything medical. I could go on for weeks cataloging all the things I don't know, but you get the idea.

How does this apply? Those scientists who produced false results about smoking, for instance, were in fact scientists, just not in the relevant fields. They were alumni of NASA's predecessor agency, the National Advisory Committee on Aeronautics, in the pre-space days and the Manhattan Project, which produced the first atomic bomb. What nuclear fission and rocketry had to do with this new field, involving human physiology and the various toxins in cigarettes, was nothing. That didn't stop them from producing paper after paper claiming in essence that black was white, that tobacco was innocent if not actually health-giving. Or from moving forward to write other papers citing each other in a continuous chain of disinformation until it became next to impossible to tease out the fact that the original results were bogus. Or that the men (and they were all men) who produced them were frauds. Because of them, the 1964 surgeon general's report on tobacco and health was forestalled for over a decade, and even when it appeared, it was doubted because of the dust they had thrown in America's eyes. The sudden drop in smoking that terrified the tobacco industry in 1952 so much that they hired agents of confusion would be reversed within a year of their efforts and not return to such a low level for twenty years, until 1972. The moral of the story is that a concerted effort to deceive can achieve results in twelve months but an authoritative report can take eight years to overcome that earlier damage. Or maybe forever.

This parable of corruption is extreme, but it points to one thing that even amateurs can do: look at the source of information. Most of the junk science that has wrecked modern life has come from people without the proper qualifications. If, as writers, we use the work of persons with the right credentials, we stand a much better chance of relying on correct information. During the COVID-19 crisis that began in 2020, the experts in virology and immunology were nearly all aligned in their understanding of the disease as facts emerged about it. The wild claims and rabid opposition to the official information came, when we could even identify its sources, from politicians with something to gain or lose, radio talk-show hosts, pillow salesmen, engineers, and doctors in unrelated fields. A chiropractor may have his or her virtues, but those do not include degrees in immunology. For that matter, many false claims came from nowhere specific but merely showed up in the murkier portions of social media, suggesting that they came from disinformation specialists, often residing in places closer to Moscow, Russia, than Moscow, Idaho.

Another strategy for sorting our sources is to watch for phrases that indicate a distance between the source and facts. One favorite claim of fraudsters is that "someone is making money." It can be useful to follow the money, if we follow it and not our vague suspicions. Arguments against climate change often claim that scientists are "getting rich" by pushing the climate change agenda. It is true that a great deal of money has been handed out in grants for study in this field, but that money has many strings attached as to how it can be spent and how it must be accounted for. There is never a line-item called "self-enrichment." On the other hand, during their decades of fighting the science and in some cases hiding the results of their own research, the extractive industries—coal and petroleum—have made trillions of dollars in profits, something those who attack the science conveniently forget. If you're going to follow the money, make sure it's money that really matters.

Similarly, claims that something "must be true" or that "people say" or even "everyone says" are weak arguments. The truth is that "people" say everything possible. I have some reasonably close friends whose opinions I would not take on any subject on earth. Or in space. There is one acquaintance who is like a heat-seeking missile for conspiracy theories. He has never trusted anything official or orthodox in his life. All a conspiracy theory needs to do is attack authority in some form, and that's good enough for him. When I hear "people say," his image floats before my eyes, which is disconcerting when he is already present in the flesh. And when I hear "everyone says," my one thought is that the speaker needs a wider circle of acquaintances, a larger "everyone." There is nothing that "everyone" says, and that includes "good morning."

These last examples are couched in the negative: don't do this, avoid that. A positive step you can take when evaluating sources is to make sure their sources are trustworthy. In general, that means asking if the sources they rely on are authoritative. It may be popular to attack expertise as "elitist," but such bias plays into the hands of fraudsters and malicious entities. When the British doctor (who was not a professional researcher) whose fraudulent study claimed a link between childhood immunizations and autism, many people flocked to the story as an explanation for their child's malady. When the medical authorities discredited his "research," many of those same people said, "See! We knew *they'd* be against him!" For them, that proved—and for many continues to prove—that his results were valid and the evil establishment shut him down for some nefarious reasons. When the medical society stripped him of his medical license, that only made him a martyr for his adherents. The truth, however, is that from study design, if any, to final paper, he sought to prove a predetermined outcome (he had tried before with a link between measles and autism, but even he couldn't pretend causality) and bent every inconvenient fact to suit his narrative. In other words, the medical authorities were right from the beginning. Even so, all these years later, I know more than one person who refuses to accept the reality of this situation. And they tend to be very vocal on social media.

This same impulse is why a twenty-four-year-old Romanian was able to sway many minds during the 2016 American presidential election. He was responsible for some of the most effective—and false—stories on social media. And why some entity calling itself "Q" has garnered a wide circle of followers who believe the deranged tales that that person or group has concocted. Many Americans are so programmed to mistrust authority that they are easily misled by anyone with a juicy story and a bad attitude. Real science, real election results, real public opinion polls are never as appealing or sexy as made-to-order tales of official or expert malfeasance.

But you don't have to rely on such wild conspiracy theories, nor on sources that rely on them. How can you judge the quality of the research behind the book or article you're reading? Notice whom or what they cite. For books, check the index or bibliography (if provided). For other sources, just pay attention as you read to how they marshal their support. It really isn't that hard.

Do experts always agree? Always get it right? Of course not. But one thing you notice if you follow, as I sometimes have, academic arguments, which by definition are between two or more people with expertise, is that both sides will be using credible information from trusted sources—and using it in good faith. That credible information can sometimes be contradictory or put to opposing uses causes confusion in some quarters, which leads some people to reject experts and facts altogether. It doesn't help that much of that information is well above the pay grade of nearly all of us, as is the case with disputes over the origin of the universe or the intricacies of the atom. That failure on our part to grasp the ins and outs of specialized fields does not mean, however, that the disputants are making it all up. Were we (by which I mean I) more capable, we could see that each party can be basing its argument on a solid foundation but that the field itself can contain contradictions, which is true of a great deal of reality.

Humans have trouble with uncertainty, nuance, imprecision, and paradox. Not to mention math. So we tend to avoid messiness, particularly if it involves numbers, in favor of simple solutions, something the enemies of truth exploit. Providing simple answers can give a leg up to false narratives if only because readers or viewers are worn out by complexities. As writers, we owe it to those who might read us to seek truth, no matter how messy or awkward. We can choose to spread light or add to the darkness. I know which I prefer.

20

Revision: It Ain't Pretty, But...

*I have rewritten—often several times—every word I
have ever published. My pencils outlast their erasers.*
—VLADIMIR NABOKOV

YOU HAVE FINISHED YOUR draft, and it's perfect. How could it
not be? You sweated and agonized over every word. You lost sleep.
You even skipped *The Simpsons*. Here's the hard part: now, blow
it up. Take it apart mentally if not physically (although I know
people who write each paragraph on a separate sheet and move
them around). Revision is, literally, about reseeing what you've
done, about looking at it from a different angle or with new eyes.
It's surprising what you see. This stage isn't about punctuation—
what does a comma matter in a paragraph that might be ripped
out? Instead, it's about making something new and improved
from work you didn't think could get better. But it can.

A few chapters ago I mentioned the three-day wait before
looking at a piece of writing. This is easy to do with the short
exercises we were discussing in those chapters. Do a different

exercise tomorrow and a different one again the day after, and then you can consider going back to that first model. Here's why: in the first seventy-two hours after we write *anything*, most of us are incapable of being sufficiently cold-blooded to do what may be required, up to and including utter destruction. We suffered too much getting to that completed draft to be able to do what must be done. On day one, I can't even see the words I have written; if I read back over it, my eyes glaze over with the love of the newborn. Each day after is a little better, and day three is when I become divorced from the project enough to see it with clarity. Meanwhile, the world is full of other things to work on.

I heard that! No, you won't have forgotten it, but you will have moved on. Other thoughts on other subjects will have happened, at a rate something on the order of hundreds per day. Not all will have been momentous, which is why you don't believe you have them that often, but you probably do. And you may even have already thought of things you wish you had said when you were a couple of days younger, or of things that occur to you with the greater wisdom of age. Because of comparatively minor changes, your perspective will have changed, if only a little, so going back to the earlier work will give you brand-new vision to see what was good and what was less so. If you prefer, it will bring you to revision. Which brings us to something almost like a maxim:

Revision = time + attention

Here is something I know: writing is never static. And that is because writers are never static. The person who can write something substantial that requires no revision or rewriting is one-in-a-million, if that common. And may be more illusion than substance. The literary critic Harold Bloom was famous for writing in a reclining chair with a felt-tipped pen on a yellow legal pad and *never revising*. No cross-outs, no overwrites. First-draft perfection, the holy grail of writing! We had a young visiting colleague one year who had been the great man's assistant, and she swore up and down that he worked in exactly that manner. I don't believe it. Or rather, I believe he did it. I don't believe it was a first draft. Without doubt, Bloom was a prodigy or genius or whatever term we care to apply to such people. If we grant that, and I do, there is a small but non-zero chance that he did indeed pour out perfection. I would argue, however, that what he really did was carry around the ideas in his head for a certain period of days working it over, holding it up to the light to examine it from each side, so that when he finally sat down to compose, what came out was the only draft but by no means the first. In saying this, I am not denigrating the achievement. Try that routine sometime: walk around for a few days obsessing on the essay or article or short story you are about to write until you have it in perfect form, and then sit down and write a single, perfect draft. It needs to be because Bloom's, however he marshaled his thoughts, were phenomenal. As I said, he was a prodigy or genius or whatever.

I work in much that fashion, with a great deal of work done before my fingers hit the keyboard. My drafts? Not perfect. Don't get me wrong. I am fortunate enough to be closer to finished form than a lot of people are, chiefly because I so despise rewriting that I spend vastly more mental energy at the front end. I want my drafts to be perfect. They are not. Take this chapter as a case in point. It has taken a week and a half or a bit more (my record keeping is somewhere south of obsessive) to write the first draft. Some of that stems from external delays, obligations I had to other ventures, such as lining up virtual classroom visits. Some of it arose from when I got stuck and started another chapter or two while I cleared my head. Sometimes I just sat and stared at my laptop as if it were a recalcitrant child refusing to produce what I commanded it to. Mostly, though, I have a limited useful creative period each day. At this point in my life, two or three hours a day is about all I can muster. On a really good day, I might produce a thousand words, or about four typed pages. (By the way, if one did produce a "puny" thousand words every day, a book first draft would emerge in two and a half months. Seventy-five days = seventy-five thousand words. That's a book. Don't sneer at modest production.) Most days are not "really good." Because of my rate of production, my three-day waiting periods are virtually guaranteed. I go back through what I have already written to sort of slot myself back into the work, and the earliest work is usually at least three days old. Not only that, but when I wasn't happy with an impasse in this chapter, I skipped over to another one about which I had a glimmer of an idea and then piddled around with it for a day or two before going back.

And what is the result of all this delayed decision-making? Some passages get cut forever. Some get moved to other chapters or held for a rainy day—and it rains a lot around here. Occasionally, the chapter makes clear that something I had thought belonged in an earlier chapter has to be taken from *there* and brought *here*. Or that a passage that was burning a hole in my writing pocket to get into this chapter has no business in it. Maybe it moves to a different one, or maybe it goes away for good.

So far this discussion has been airborne, looking down on reworking a manuscript from a great height, which is to say from where things look pretty easy. What does revision look like at ground level? Usually like a pain in the butt. It involves several steps, each just as painful as the one before. Other writers may have a different list, but this is mine.

- **Fall out of love with your writing.** You have to love and nurture a piece of writing in the composing stage, but that love will undermine your efforts to revise and edit.
- **Reread the entire piece.** Resist the temptation to edit, rewrite, or otherwise act on anything you find. Just read straight through; there will be time enough for those other actions later. Your reading time will be dictated by the length of the piece you're working on, which explains why I revise one chapter at a time. For this pass, concentrate on the *feel* of your draft. Does it seem to say everything it needs to? Are there parts that feel too long or not long enough? Are there parts out of place? Make notes in the margins of anything to fix, but keep moving.
- **Fix anything having to do with structure while the rereading is fresh in your mind.** This is a terrible place for another three-day gap. Start shuffling things around to a preferred order. The changes can be small or immense. Sometimes you have to create whole sections or, more agonizingly, excise them. Other times, the job is easier and all that is required is moving parts around a little. I once submitted a manuscript about American literature. Each chapter after the introduction was about a single book. When it landed on my editor's desk, he saw (as I had, although I pretended not to) that the chapter on *The Wonderful Wizard of Oz* had to go in favor of one

not yet written on a different book that really was more important. I had my reasons for my original choice, but I couldn't fight him on the decision. I did, however, feel ill as I ripped out my chapter and even worse when I read the replacement book and wrote the new chapter. That novel was *Moby-Dick*, one of the central books of the American experience but also a monster. It had not been a favorite when I read it for class decades earlier. There was a bright side: I liked the novel far more than my twenty-year-old self had, and the resulting chapter was praised by reviewers as one of the best. Even so, the switch was awful. I really had loved that *Oz* chapter!

Having rearranged the furniture, it is time to get inside paragraphs. Read them singly and stay inside the one you're working on until you finish it. Then move to the next. Make sure that the paragraph is a unified whole, that it is unified *and* complete. If it is really two ideas, split it into two paragraphs. If unfinished, finish it. Is the main idea (often called the *topic sentence*) easy to find? Does it lay out the idea effectively? Are the supporting sentences in their best order?

Make things flow. If you didn't do this in your draft (and hardly anyone does), insert transitions where you need them—between sentences, paragraphs, ideas, or chapters. You will have noticed in your rereading a clunk when your continuity is broken by a new subject without any connecting material. In a longer work, by which I mean more than a few pages, those clunks register like seams in an expressway: thump, thump, thump, thump. That sound breaks the illusion of continuity and control,

that "vivid and continuous dream" that John Gardner
tells us about. Get rid of any thumping.

- **Lather, rinse, repeat.** Just because you have completed your revision and even your rewrite, that doesn't
  mean you're done revising. Thoughts will continue to
  assail you about improving your manuscript; some will
  even be good ideas. Follow up on every idea you have that
  isn't born of self-loathing. At this stage, you have to be on
  the lookout for that Watcher at the Gate who tries to tell
  you that your work stinks. This step won't take as long as
  the initial revision, but those late changes can improve
  your writing greatly.

At this point you will be having one of two thoughts, either
"how can I fall out of love with my writing when I didn't like it
in the first place" or "my writing is precious to me, so how can I
fall out of love with it?" Whichever response you have, they are
born of the same wellspring of feelings, that love-hate relationship
we have with writing, both the act itself and the products of the
act. Love or hate what you have just produced (three days ago,
remember), you need to look at it dispassionately, as if it is the
work of a stranger. This takes some mental gymnastics. Of course
you wrote it. You can't forget that, but what you can do is develop
a spot in your mind that you train to handle the unpleasant task
of dismantling what you so lovingly (or distastefully) assembled.
The creative mind and the critical mind are two separate entities, although there will always be a struggle between them for
supremacy. Just as the Watcher is an aspect of the overactive—or
premature—critical faculty during the creative process, so the
inability to turn off (or at least down) the creative mind, which

contains more than a little ego, will inhibit your efforts to turn your draft into a finished piece of writing. In my experience, it is equally hard to tell the Watcher to bugger off and to order your creative impulse to pipe down. It requires practice and renewed attention each time you write or polish. Even at that, you never win; the best you can hope for is a reasonably stable standoff.

Once you conquer the ego-monster, reread. Yes, the whole piece. My friend Jim Cash used to read however much he had of his screenplay every morning before starting the day's writing. A completed screenplay runs (or did, when movies were closer to two hours) about 120 pages, so when he got near the end of a script, the reading really cut into the writing time. The good news was that he didn't have much left to write. The other good news was that he wasn't writing Victorian novels. For your revision process, this stage is just a general review. You're on the lookout for anything, structurally speaking, that jars, clangs, or clatters. We tend to think that the parts that follow this paragraph are *real* revision because they feel like *doing*, but there is no step in the revision process more real than that initial rereading.

Before the rereading can fade from memory, which it does with surprising speed, start the Big Fix. Start on the broadest scale: ideas and how they are expressed, movement between parts, the shapeliness of the whole. Move anything that seems out of order, cut extraneous discussions, punch up any parts that seem underdeveloped, and make sure your logic is, well, logical.

Having made the global improvements, get progressively more granular. First, move inside the paragraphs, making sure their structure is solid. A well-constructed paragraph is like a mini-essay: it develops an idea (part of the bigger one, if we are doing things properly) from initial statement (or sometimes question) through the key points so that readers feel that they have learned or experienced something in just this one small part. Having satisfied yourself that the parts are in the best order, *do not leave*. Stay in this paragraph until you have finished the job. If you must leave—because you are stuck on wording in one place, for instance—highlight the paragraph as needing more work. You would be surprised at how easy it is to forget to go back to a trouble spot that you couldn't possibly forget. Move straight to fixing individual sentences. You've got them in the right order, so make each one as perfect as you can. While you're at it, make sure they have some variety. You want some simple sentences, some compound sentences (ones that link shorter sentences together with commas and conjunctions), and occasional complex sentences (where one of the possible short sentences is changed into a dependent clause, one that by adding or changing a word becomes incapable of standing independently). Writing is nearly always better when rhythms and lengths are varied a bit.

While you're messing around in those paragraphs, try to make them connect smoothly from one to the next. When we're inexperienced writers, transitions just seem like stumbling blocks strewn in our path. We work so hard just to capture what we want to say that going beyond that to smooth the reader's journey seems superfluous, like so many frills. Frilly, transitions are not. They are as essential to good writing as subject-verb-object. They help even out the bumps, and the higher the bumps or the more distance between them, the more work transitions need to do. And if the gaps are in logic, you really need transitions to fill in or the result will be ugly. Think of it like walls in a house. A wall is supposed to appear continuous and unblemished from one corner to the next. The trouble is, walls are composed of sheets of drywall that are only four feet wide. Got a lot of four-foot walls in your house? Neither do I. So everywhere two sheets of drywall meet, finishers apply a special tape and a sort of mortar called drywall compound. When that compound dries, they sand and smooth until you can't tell where the seams really are. If you can tell, that's bad workmanship.

So, what about this "lather, rinse, repeat" business? Do you mean we have to do it all again?

Just so. The mere fact that you have revised according to your best estimate doesn't mean that the piece is finished, only that you're tired of it. Go through it again and find what you didn't realize you had missed before. Here's the process:

1. Read the manuscript again. Fix any issues you find.
2. Reread it again and again until you want to scream.
3. Scream.
4. Get to work on the final revision.

Only when you reach the point where any potential change makes the manuscript worse will you have finished revising it.

Oh, and there is a step 5 when you finish. Lay your head on the seatback and apply ice. I recommend a package of frozen peas inside a resealable bag. They are almost infinitely reusable and conform to foreheads, ankles, elbows, and pretty much any other body part far better than ice cubes or traditional ice bags. You will have earned it.

Remember this: revision is not something writing teachers force students to do out of sadism. They know, rather, that it is the single most important element in producing accomplished, clean, professional prose. All the brilliant ideas in the world can't hold up against lousy revising and editing.

21

Detailing Your Prose (2)

If it sounds like writing, I rewrite it.
—ELMORE LEONARD

OKAY, YOU'VE SWEATED AND slaved over drafts and revisions, and you are bursting with desire to be finished with your project. *Now* you can fret the commas, also the periods, the spelling, the wording, all that trifling stuff that turns out to matter quite a lot. Whatever *How to Write Like a Writer* is, it is not a usage handbook, for a host of reasons. Mostly, we have been having a lovely time together, and I don't want to spoil the mood by throwing around a lot of "thou shalts" and, worse, "thou shalt nots." Also, however, this book is pushing up against the upper length limit for a writing text. You may even feel it blew right past that limit.

The thing is, usage books and style manuals are long, sometimes *really* long. My old copy of the *MLA Handbook* (MLA standing for Modern Language Association, the professional organization for college English and foreign language teachers and students) clocks in at just over 300 pages. *The Chicago Manual of*

Style, which most publishers follow, pushes the scale even harder with 1,146 pages in the latest edition obeying the lure of gravity. And just to show how these things can get out of hand, the original *MLA Style Sheet* from 1951 (revised 1970) was a mere 28 pages. Twenty-eight. *The Chicago Manual* was already 762 pages in my thirteenth edition from 1982. Much of the bloat in each of these involves the innumerable nuances in citing sources and compiling bibliographies, which I hope will not be your lot in life as it has been in mine. For comparison, William Strunk Jr. wrote a pamphlet called *The Elements of Style* for his students at Cornell University in 1919 at a mere 43 pages, enlarged by 9 pages the following year. Evidently, there were some things he forgot to mention. When one of his former pupils, *Charlotte's Web* author E. B. White, expanded it in 1959, it remained a slim 71 pages. Even so, would you like this book to be seventy or so pages more? Yeah, neither would I.

The second major reason not to discuss usage in a book like this (all right, in this book) is that usage practices change more rapidly than ever before because of a host of forces. Mostly, because of the internet. That's our excuse for everything, right? Usually, when we say that about language change, we mean online communication and social media practices. Let me give you one example: the direct-address comma. For my whole life and long before it, when we address someone directly, we have used a comma before the name, as in "Happy birthday, Bill" or "Hi, Andy." A highly unscientific examination of salutations on emails (over, say, the last twenty years) and Facebook birthday greetings (ten years or so) suggests that the comma in those constructions packed its bags and left for Tahiti. Right from the beginning of the Emailocene, that comma was absent. I used it for about a month and, abashed at how fussy it seemed, dropped it for good. I sometimes use it in reply to someone who uses it in writing first. Someone like my editor, who now knows my secret. Otherwise, no comma. I still use the comma in birthday greetings, so in my examples Bill gets a comma and Andy doesn't. That comma also belongs if we use not a name but a status, as in, "Happy birthday, brother!" Which would apply to them both.

As much as it pains me to say this, you really don't need me for this part. There is a wealth of websites and books on usage, all of them more comprehensive than my book can be. Many are free, always a plus. Better still, since they are addressable online, the information you need is as close as your phone. The most all-inclusive are the websites run by college writing centers, of which probably the most famous is the Online Writing Laboratory (OWL) at Purdue University. As with so much in modern life, branding is critical, and there is a certain advantage for people like me to be able to say to students, "Check OWL." Beyond that bit of marketing brilliance, the site is wondrously helpful. In addition to the advice they hand out to their charges about how to begin and develop and wrap up writing assignments (their reason for being, after all), OWL and others like it offer explanations of the contents of the various style guides, particularly MLA and American Psychological Association (APA, which is used in most science, technical, and social science fields) models, as well as a rationale for the existence of style guides in the first place. As I wrote this book, OWL had a message that its "student content developers" were busy "reviewing and updating" its MLA information to bring the site into conformity with the recently released *MLA Handbook Ninth Edition*. Other sources may offer help with *The Chicago Manual of Style* or *The Associated Press*

Stylebook, which is the bible of journalistic writing. The point here is that pretty much everything you need to know about how to format writing and write for various audiences is available for the price of a Google search, which is far less expensive than the style guides themselves.

Almost from the beginning of writing, there have been books published to tell readers that they're doing it all wrong. There is probably a clay tablet buried in a cave somewhere declaring that none of the Mycenaean Greeks know how to write *Linear B* script anymore, and here is the right way. Your local library or bookstore can open a world of writing improvement for writers. We have already noted *The Elements of Style* as a classic in the general writing and usage category, and *Fowler's Modern English Usage* is another, 2015 bringing a fourth edition of what began as *A Dictionary of Modern English Usage* (1926) by H. W. Fowler. Both are highly prescriptive—do this, don't do that, and for heaven's sake, don't even consider that one—and not entirely to contemporary tastes. Harvard linguist and cognitive psychologist Steven Pinker seeks to address this shortcoming with *The Sense of Style: The Thinking Person's Guide to Writing in the 21st Century* (2014), using his knowledge of language and the mind to blaze a trail forward.

In other words, there is no shortage of books and online resources on how to deploy words and tiny marks to best advantage. Many of them, like Lynne Truss's improbable 2003 bestseller, *Eats, Shoots & Leaves*, are my-way-or-the-highway prescriptive. At least she gives us fair warning in her subtitle, *The Zero Tolerance Approach to Punctuation*. And she is quite entertaining in her diacritical hectoring. Because there are so many useful aids to usage, I see no point in lingering over comma splices (even though they are a favorite topic) or run-on sentences.

That said, there are some topics we can discuss about how to look at your next-to-final draft to examine all the fit-and-finish items that require attention. The first one is clarity. You owe it to your readers—and ultimately to yourself—to be as clear as possible without becoming tedious. I picked up my local paper recently to confront a story about a family of three being attacked by a man with a weapon more suited to forestry than homicide. In any case, the good news is that all three survived, but that's not *our* immediate concern. Pronouns are, specifically the vague and confusing uses of them. The story contains two adult males, each of whom can be referred to as "the man" (which is not a pronoun but acts a good deal like one here) as well as "he" and "him." Which they are, with no specific identification when the reporter switches from one "him" to the other. It turned out that when the attacker grew weary of ax-swinging, he pulled out a gun, firing repeatedly before the gun jammed. At this point, the male victim took action, and the narrative becomes a jumble of references to "he" and "him" and "the man," as in the following sentence, "When he glanced back at the man, he saw that he still had the gun and was moving, the father said." Wait, what? Or rather, who? The real problem is that as usage in this vein continues, confusion escalates.

In this article, the writer would have been well-served to use more specific nouns—the attacker, the assailant, the victim, the father—which she does some, but not frequently enough. The first "he" here is innocent; it has a specific referent late in the prior sentence, so that one can stay. But the morass would be less morass-y with more detail. "When he glanced back at the man, he saw that his attacker still had the gun and was moving, the father said." In this case, both uses of "he" refer to the father/victim, and each comes with an active verb ("he glanced"/"he saw"). Sometimes, though, we are best served to change the sentence structure, "Glancing back at his attacker, he saw that the man still had the gun and was moving." There are nearly always more ways than one to skin a sentence, and our first effort is not necessarily the best. Writers (and by this, I mean me) are too often satisfied that we are being clear simply because we know what we meant to say. When we step outside our own self-contained thought loop and ask how things look to outsiders, we realize that the only clear fact is our own muddiness. I try to take that step away whenever I use a pronoun (you know who they are) or a generic noun (man, woman, outsider, reader), and if you have been paying attention, you will realize how often I fail to follow my own precept on this point. Still, our best is all we can do. Just remember:

Proper care and feeding of readers demands that we avoid misunderstandings whenever we can.

This example points up a basic truth: your grammar checker is never to be trusted with the nuances of writing. Why? Because even the most sophisticated grammar program can only detect obvious errors in the prose, so if something is not a clear and obvious mistake, the program will not pick it up. Every use of "man," "he," and "him" was correct in its own local place in the sentences. The little grammar gremlin, seeing the *syntax* (placement of words within the statement) was correct, would pass those right by in its relentless search for gaffes.

I spend a certain portion of my writing life cursing the gremlins for their incorrect, misleading, and frequently idiotic suggestions. I can't tell you how often the Grammar feature in Microsoft

Word has tried to change my verb to match the object of the preposition immediately in front of it and not the true subject of the sentence four or five words earlier. It is following a rule as it understands it (which is to say, as it was programmed to understand it), but it is incapable of seeing the bigger linguistic picture. What I do know is how immeasurably worse my writing would be if I accepted every suggestion the gremlins sent my way. Why is that? The rules for identifying errors must be programmed into the algorithm. Tell me, just who do you think writes those algorithms? Linguistics professors? Not on your life. Some person or persons, no doubt bright and perfectly competent in their own field (coding, which has its own special grammar), are writing received rules as they understand them. The question is: How well do they understand them? The probable answer is, only slightly better than I understand JavaScript, and I understand it to the extent that I know it exists.

The best instruments for polishing your manuscript are not your eyes but your ears. Mostly.

Let me say at the outset that this statement may not apply to readers who have been hearing-impaired from birth. I do not know if they develop some compensating *feel* for how language works in the absence of hearing how words fit together. My experience with deaf students was extremely limited, although the few I did have wrote as well as anyone else in my classes. I do know that, having grown up as a hearing person, my own partial hearing loss has not affected my ability with auditory editing.

There are, of course, places in your writing where the ears-over-eyes assertion will let you down, including one very special exception: "who" and "whom." We could do the same for "lie" and "lay," but that dog done died. Actually, it was murdered, unequivocally and finally, by Bob Dylan in his 1969 classic "Lay Lady Lay." The distinction had been on its deathbed for a while (as in, between a few and many decades) prior to the song's release, but with "lay" receiving the imprimatur of the singer-of-the-decade and voice-of-his-generation, its fate was sealed. Grammarians decried the desecration of a beloved sacred cow (beloved of grammarians if not the rest of America, which has never had all that great a handle on the distinction), but to no avail. Don't, as an entirely different song reminds us, spit into the wind.

But back to "who" and "whom." This is one time you can't trust . . . anyone. Your parents set a terrible example. Your great-aunt—no, not that aunt, the other one who thought that horehound was an actual candy flavor—seemed to think that "whom" was simply a more elegant formulation of "who" and therefore sprinkled it liberally where it didn't belong. Your third-grade teacher may have been someone's great-aunt, given her frequent application of the wrong one. Your friends? Ha! Forget it. Actually, you know who you can trust? The Who, that's who. They set an excellent model for the rest of us by placing "who" in its proper and noble position up front: "Who's Next," "Who Are You," and the late "Who." I'll admit the last one is grammatically shaky, lacking any other words, but the principle is sound: "who" is the subject form (the *nominative* case, if you want the high-class term) of the pronoun. As such, it will appear at the beginning of sentences and noun clauses and titles, as in "Who ate my Snickers bar?" The native English speaker over the age of three who would ask, "Whom ate my Snickers bar?" has never existed. Rack my brain as I might, I cannot come up with a sentence wherein "whom" (as opposed to "whomever," which can and once in a very great while does begin a sentence) appears at the front without quotation marks around it to indicate the item in question is the word itself and not a person, as with "'Whom' is frequently misused."

You know who else you can't trust? Authors. In 1976, Richard Lathrop published his book on creative and active job-seeking, *Who's Hiring Who*. It set my teeth on edge then and, now in its eighth edition, it still does. I bought a copy decades ago and found it interesting but ultimately had to banish it from my shelves to avoid the inevitable dental damage. By rights, the title should be *Who's Hiring Whom*, but that lacks a certain punch. Lathrop may have been worried that readers would be turned off by his putting on airs. Imagine, an author using proper grammar! Says the guy with multiple titles that use "like" where "as" would be the traditional and correct choice. Be that as it may, at this late date, I suspect the number of Americans who would be untroubled by "who's hiring who" hovers at around ninety percent, maybe higher. As a matter of usage, "whom" belongs anywhere that a grammatical object is called for—direct object, indirect object, prepositional object. Seems simple enough, right? But here's where it gets weird. In English, objects of the preposition can be noun clauses with verbs and everything; that means that what looks to be serving as an *object* is really the *subject* of a clause, the whole of which is the true object of the preposition. I know, I know. Just keep in mind that "who's hiring whom" or maybe "To whom it may concern" is the correct, simple form while we complicate matters. You might have occasion to ask, "What is the appropriate punishment for whoever tore down the town gazebo?" Not likely, but you might. And if you did, you might be tempted to use "whomever," because that is the object form (known as the *accusative* case among linguists), and it has a preposition right in front of it. But the pronoun by itself is not the object of "for." That would be the entire phrase, "whoever tore down the town gazebo," and "whomever tore down the town gazebo" just sounds wrong. Because it is.

The Comma Queen—also known as Mary Norris, who spent her career at *The New Yorker* correcting the tiny and not-so-tiny mistakes that even writers at that august venue make in their prose—offered a "simple solution" in a 2018 article in that magazine. Her solution? When in doubt, substitute "she" and "her" for the more mysterious pronouns. The logic is that we almost never make mistakes with the female personal pronouns, so the correct choice is easy, at which we can swap "who" back in for "she" and "whom" for "her." I like it as far as it goes, but the solution I proposed in class for decades is to use "he" and "him" to do the swaps. My reason is not that I'm a male chauvinist pig (that's for others to say) but that both "he" and "who" end in vowels, "him" and "whom" in "m," so there is less room for confusion. Either solution will work, although you have to allow for those weird prepositional phrases where substitutions are impossible, English having quite thoughtlessly failed to provide us with "(s)he-ever" to swap for "whoever."

The ear problem is also true of "you and I," mostly due to a blue million pop songs (or maybe the same one a blue million times) that employ the auditory-nerve-shredding "between you and I." I blame The Doors, even if their lyric was not "between" but "for you and I" in "Touch Me." Remember, this is the subject form, and "me" will nearly always be the object of the preposition ("for," "between," "with"). Now you've heard Rascal Flatts,

Britney Spears, Demi Lovato, and who knows how many others croon some version of "[preposition] you and I," and your hearing is permanently damaged. It can't be helped and may well change in the near future, which is one of many things that make me thankful that we are not saddled with immortality. I don't want to see the day when that construction is correct.

On the whole, however, your ears are your friends. You have been hearing whole sentences your entire life and speaking them for nearly as long. You know when a sentence has reached (or should have) its end without the benefit of seeing punctuation. Not only that, you can hear when a plural subject and a singular verb form, one that usually although by no means always ends in "s," should not consort with each other. In fact, there's a sort of mnemonic that addresses this situation: if the noun doesn't end in an "s," the verb does. Which is swell if we ignore all the exceptions. Such as this:

> "That guy *plays* loud music." / "Those guys *play* loud music."

So far, so good, but what about:

> "That *man* plays loud music." / "Those *men* play loud music."

The slogan doesn't account for nouns that don't end in "s" in their plural forms. Maybe it should say, "If the noun doesn't end in an 's,' the verb does, if both noun and verb are regular." Some memory assistant that is. It's fine, though, because your ears are better than any rule at accounting for irregular nouns and verbs.

You don't need a rule or a mnemonic for most usage questions. That's what ears are for. When in doubt, do what sounds right. You'll make some mistakes that way, but fewer than you think.

Since we're talking about the polishing stage of writing, there are things that your eyes are likely to miss but your ears never will—which is why you need to make your last pass through your manuscript oral. Yes, it's awkward and embarrassing, but it must be done. Get over your hang-ups and read the thing out loud. Here's why.

You mistype any number of common function words—articles, prepositions, that sort of thing in two, three, and four letters. If you're like me, there are predictable pairs of troublemakers. In my case, they include "of/if," "of/or/on," "and/at," "be/me," and "me/my." They are all common errors among those who practice touch-typing. I do not mix up these words in usage or in my mind or anywhere that my fingers are not involved. Those criminal digits, on the other hand, seem to delight in twisting my intentions. Sometimes I think they do it on purpose. Every one of those words, you will notice, is perfectly spelled. That has two implications: first, that spellcheckers will not "see" anything amiss, and second, that neither will your very own eyes. Hard to see anything wrong with perfectly spelled words. On the other hand, if you meant, for instance, "if" but typed "of," your ears are going to hear that as all kinds of wrong.

Look, your job as writer is to make your final manuscript as clean as it can be. That means that the final pass is an all-hands-on-deck job for your skills and your senses. If smelling the thing helped, I'd say sniff it all over. As things stand, we only have your eyes and ears and innate good sense. **As always, your main ques-**

tion should be: How can I make this best for my readers? For me, that means making sure that every series has a comma before the last item and conjunction—that thing that is called the "Oxford comma" by people who want to dismiss it as needless and too uptight and "series comma" by those of us who want to eliminate confusion. Here's why I use it: while ninety-five or so percent of the time it isn't needed, there is no instance where it will make things less clear and a few where it can make them more so. Academic and publishing style manuals—*The MLA Handbook*, *The Chicago Manual of Style*, and *The Publication Manual of the American Psychological Association*—require its use. The Associated Press, always interested in brevity, leaves it out. Here's why I use it (aside from those sacred texts): "I delight in my children, Queen Latifah and Bo Diddley." I really want to avoid questions as to why I named my kids "Queen Latifah" and "Bo Diddley," which is one way that can be read without that series comma. Better to be understood as being a punctuation fussbudget than as being cruel to children. But go ahead and do what you think best.

Lest you think that I'm not fair-minded, there is one feature for which grammar checker programs are well-suited, and this is the only reason I leave mine open: they are demons at finding doubled words. If I were to write "doubled doubled words," grammar check would be all over it. And is, as I look at my screen.

Throughout this discussion I have emphasized your duty to your reader during the revising and polishing phase. But we should also remember our duty to the writing itself and by extension to our earlier selves. This thing, this piece of writing, is the product of your mind, your labors to bring it into being. You worked hard on that for hours or days or months or however long. Now that you've successfully produced a workable final draft, what does it say about your commitment if you decide that slipshod final proofreading and editing is good enough? Just how much did you care about not only the product but the work you poured into it? How much self-respect do you have? It is a fact of life that we judge work in part by appearance. No one is going to sway readers by cosmetic perfection if the argument is lousy; you have to produce something of quality in the first place. If the argument is good but the polishing is weak, on the other hand, readers may conclude that you just don't care all that much. There was an old advertising slogan for a greeting card company, "when you care enough to send the very best." If you really care, and you should, given how hard you have worked up to the final pass, you really ought to keep on caring till the end. You do, of course, but we humans have a funny way of showing our care sometimes. Let's face it, writing wears us out, and the last leg of that race is a contest between will and exhaustion. Don't let exhaustion win. Even if you're just firing off a letter to the editor, take a few moments to clean up any unsightly gaffes. Show readers your best. That way, you'll show your respect for them and your work. They both deserve it.

Conclusion

The Exquisite Pain of Never Being Quite Finished

We are all apprentices in a craft where no one ever becomes a master.

—ERNEST HEMINGWAY

MICHIGAN, WHERE I HAVE spent my adult life, has something of a college sports rivalry. The head football coach of one huge school said of the rivalry and resentment toward the other, "It's not over. It'll never be over." I have bad news for aspiring writers: your task, your avocation, your career will be like that. No matter how good an ending feels as you type the terminal punctuation, there are always unresolved issues, from little things the writer could have done better to more substantive assertions that could have been made by way of wrapping up. We do our best, but ultimately, human frailty will win out.

Speaking of his exquisite novel, *The French Lieutenant's Woman*, John Fowles said that when he finished composing it, it was one hundred thousand words long and perfect. A few days later, when he was ready to revise, "I see a hundred thousand things wrong with it." Irish poet William Butler Yeats, who was great enough to win the Nobel Prize in Literature, kept revising poems long after publication. As a result, he is one of the few modern poets to warrant a "variorum" edition of his work, which records all the changes between drafts and published versions. If writers of that cast find fault with their work, why should we be different? To be completely happy with one's work is probably to be too easily satisfied.

These days, the world is only too happy to provide writers with cause for dissatisfaction. In the original edition of *How to Read Literature Like a Professor*, among other wobbles, I mistake one Shakespeare character for another, something I repaired in the revised edition eleven years later. All good, right? Except that *four months* after the new version appeared, I heard from a woman who otherwise praised the book but wondered why, in trying to establish the difficulty of something, I used the simile "like finding a suitable partner of the opposite sex." Did I really need, she asked, to be so "heteronormative"? No, of course I didn't need to be; I wasn't thinking. Despite changes in the world and in my own thinking, I didn't notice that what was always a flippant throwaway line could easily be changed to "the preferred [or desired] sex." It would barely change the line length. So easy. So dumb. Guess what became item one of changes in any new edition? But here's the thing, in the four months from that glorious Tuesday when the book hit store shelves and the dismal Wednesday or Thursday when her email arrived, I had already spotted things that now seemed less than ideal. I have three periods of euphoria in the process of writing and publishing a book: the day I sign a contract, the day I submit the manuscript to my editor, and publication day. The first lasts twenty-four hours, at which point I realize the magnitude of the task ahead of me and get to work. The second lasts until the day I get an email from my editor with a heavily marked-up manuscript attached, which signals another period of arduous labor. The last one finds me walking on air for about two weeks, at which point I start to recall all the little things that aren't perfect. It can be a long list.

The only one of those three that every writer can experience whether published or not is the second one. There is—and absolutely deserves to be—a period of euphoria when any writing project reaches its end. You earned it; go ahead and wallow in it. But then other thoughts creep in: Was that comparison accurate? Did I say things forcefully enough or was I too forceful? Did that final paragraph do everything I wanted it to do?

A pain, right? Get used to it. There is a misconception that learning to write better will make the process go better, smoother, less error-riddled. Somehow, we're going to be able to plan and execute flawless work on the first draft, and from there we're in clover. No revision! No editing! The earthly paradise! Sorry, it won't happen. Words are stubborn things. They don't want to obey commands, so they keep saying things we didn't intend. They sound bad next to their neighbors, demanding to be changed or moved. As if that weren't enough, ideas prove equally resistant to our blandishments. They are slippery and unmanageable. Just when we think we have them in place, they open up to barely related ideas that we had no intention of going near. Or they shut down entirely and refuse to budge. It's mad, really, how difficult writing is, how obstinate it can be. I have been writing more or less continually for over fifty years, and it is as hard as ever. If I can wring out three or four pages, that's a red-letter day. Every once in a while, there's a bigger bounce, maybe six or eight pages, but that might mean the next day comes up dry. It's enough to make you believe in a muse, but one that doesn't like you all that much.

Why do we do it, then, if it's a struggle? Every writer has a different answer. I enjoy the struggle even on the bad days. Sometimes I make myself laugh out loud. If you do that and you're not writing, people worry about you. I get a kick out of finding the right phrase, something I've never said quite that way before. I get out a lot of aggression, although that had more visceral pleasure when I could hammer on a manual typewriter. And of course, I love it when a plan comes together. The book I planned and the book I write are never the same—that's a good thing. I find out in the execution what was wrong with the original design, what I didn't know when I began, what I learned that should have been obvious but wasn't. The process is educational. Humbling, too. And there's more. The first job I ever had was baling hay back when hay bales were a size that could be tossed around by teenagers. That meant I got to hang out with my friends and have a good time on the hay wagon while sweating up a storm in the sun. But it also meant that I logged plenty of time in the haymow, and you haven't lived (and nearly died) until you've worked inches from a tin roof in 90-degree heat. We took a thermometer up one day and it read 120 degrees. The rule that day was unload one wagon only and then get down from there and back out on the wagon. Now, tell me again why I should hate writing?

One of your challenges as a writer is to find your rewards. My guess is that if you write *anything* beyond what you are required to do by school or your job, you already have that answer. Perhaps you really like keeping track of your days. Or you find researching and writing your family history fulfilling. Maybe you like seeing your name in the newspaper when it's not on the police blotter. Or you find expressing yourself rewarding. Or you like the constant challenge of producing news items for your town. There are as many reasons, and combinations of reasons, for writing as there are writers. Find yours and embrace them. You'll need them on the tough days. Look, not everyone has the temperament and dedication to be a writer. For one thing, it requires an ability to sit in one place for long stretches when nothing is happening. On the other hand, that affords the freedom to stare blankly into space without being questioned about wasting time. Some of us welcome the excuse.

Which brings us to a final point before we part.

Let's get one thing straight: if you write, you are a writer. Not an "aspiring" or "would-be" writer, not someone who "hopes to become a writer," and certainly not a "failed" writer. The equation is dirt simple: if you write, you're a writer. No modifiers. An aspiring writer is somebody who sits around wishing to write something. A failed writer is a writer who gives up. Writing isn't about publication, only the act. You can even be a writer who dislikes writing; a great many professionals fall into that category. They bitch and moan about what torment writing is and then get up the next day and do it again. It is an action, not an attitude.

If you really want to confuse the punters, call yourself something more specific to the sort of writing you do. Introduce yourself as "a diarist" or "an aphorist," meaning someone who writes aphorisms (admittedly a small club), or "an epistler," or writer of epistles (letters), or whatever sort of writer you most often are. Tell me words aren't fun.

No matter what sort of writer you are, be proud of it. As I

said a long time ago, there has never been another person who would write the things you write in the way you write them. And the act of writing is one of the things that sets you apart from the ten billion or so persons who have ever existed. This is something you have chosen to do, to be, and it—you—should be celebrated. That's you: the celebrated writer.

Appendix

Bold Statements
(and Bald-Faced Truths)

THROUGHOUT THE BOOK I have assailed readers with boldface pronouncements that no doubt felt as if I was shouting at you. I may have been, but only because I wanted to make a point on something or other. As their number climbed, it seemed reasonable to abstract them out into a single location so that you don't have to wonder, "What was that thing he said way back there?" Here they are, not in the order in which they originally appeared but gathered into tribes related by subject or theme. With luck, you may find what you are looking for without having to thumb back through the entire volume.

First Principles

All writing is an act of imagination. Don't be afraid to exercise yours.

Writing is a conversation between two people, a writer and a reader.

Writing, like life, is adjustment. When changes must be made, embrace them.

Writing Basics

1. Write every day.
2. Break Rule 1 as necessary, and don't beat yourself up over it.
3. Read. Widely.
4. Know thyself.
5. Remember your readers. Always.
6. Be clear.
7. Any writing from a paragraph to a magnum opus needs a beginning, middle, and ending.
8. Obey the rules of good writing when you can; break them when you must.
9. Use your best words available in the best order.
10. When in doubt, choose the simplest word that completely explains the situation.
11. Write the best you can in the time you have.
12. Finish the job.

The Writer

You are the most important being in your writing world.

Don't hide your light.

You are not a machine.

Your writing persona must be someone you are comfortable inhabiting.

The Audience

However large your audience, you only reach them one reader at a time.

For the time that you are writing, your reader is the most important person in your life.

For every piece of writing, know (or discover) the answers to these two questions:

1. Why do my readers need to know what I am going to tell them (or how can I convince them they need to know)?

2. What do I need to do to make them happy that they read it?

Keep readers reading.

Always, your main question should be: How can I make this best for my readers?

Proper care and feeding of readers demands that we avoid misunderstandings whenever we can.

Practical Matters

For any writing project, the nature of the task dictates how information is managed.

Every piece of writing is an argument, even if its only point is, "I'm worth reading."

The writer's first goal for a piece of writing is always
to move from the initial capital letter to the final
period.

Regarding invention/prewriting: none of it is for
anyone's eyes but yours.

An opening must be your best introduction of your
subject and treatment to your audience.

For your opening: bait a hook. Reel in your readers
from the very start.

No one ever reached the end of an essay without reaching the end of the opening.

Always listen to your writing; it is talking to you with
every word you write.

Whenever possible, make the subject of your thought
the subject of your sentence.

Burn your thesaurus.

Any draft can be fixed except one that doesn't exist.

Compose, then repair, never the reverse.

Discovering what doesn't work is part of finding what
does.

Waste not, want not.

[For longer work] learn to write the pieces and then move
on to some suitable arrangement of those pieces.

Revising, Fixing, and Polishing

Revision = time + attention

While revising:

    ✎ Fall out of love with your writing.

- Reread the entire piece.
- Fix anything having to do with structure while the rereading is fresh in your mind.
- Now that you've rearranged the furniture, it is time to get inside paragraphs.
- Make things flow.
- Lather, rinse, repeat.

The best instruments for polishing your manuscript are not your eyes but your ears. Mostly.

You don't need a rule or a mnemonic for most usage questions. That's what ears are for. When in doubt, do what sounds right.

Self-evaluation needs to be not harsh, but just.

Writing is recursive. That is, the process is not a straight line but folds back and loops around.

The Seven Deadly Sins, Writers' Edition

1. Worry
2. Self-doubt
3. Overconfidence
4. Muddiness
5. Vagueness
6. Poor structure
7. Dishonesty

Acknowledgments

ONE NEVER WRITES A book like this on one's own, and I have been blessed to have had excellent instructors, colleagues, friends, and students who have taught me a very great deal about not only how we write but how we learn to write, and by extension how we learn to teach writing.

I was fortunate to come along at the moment in history when writing instruction was moving from a sort of cookbook approach toward something more research-based and nuanced. Unsurprisingly, it was the great age of the writing book. One of the great thinkers on writing instruction was Donald Murray of the University of New Hampshire and the *Boston Globe*. Working as a journalist and an English professor gave him insight into the pressures under which writers, seasoned pros, and beginners alike labor. His *Learning by Teaching* (1982) became a touchstone for a generation of us, but there is so much more. Ken Macrorie's composition text *Telling Writing* (1970) is, remarkably, still in print half a century later. I used it, along with Clinton S. Burhans's *The Would-Be Writer* (1971), another fairly early process-writing book. It seemed at one point that every university had a writing instructor with a process book. Macrorie was at Western Michigan University, Burhans at Michigan State University—where I would become a graduate student a few years later and he would be director of writing courses. I also read a number of other books with the same approach; they all preached the same main points, and any of them could work. Peter Elbow of the Massachusetts Institute of Technology, used his own difficulties in writing under traditional structures and strictures to blaze a trail for freewriting (a term he picked up from Macrorie, who wrote it as two words) as an invention technique in his 1973 *Writing Without Teachers*, a situation we can all aspire to. I always admired his iconoclasm and general rascality. Then there are the several writers and books I mention in these pages: Anne Lamott's *Bird by Bird* (1995), William Zinsser's *On Writing Well* (1976), John Gardner's *The Art of Fiction* (1983), and the peerless John McPhee's *Draft No. 4* (2018). Each, in its way, has been invaluable. The trend continues with each new generation of writing instructors. One of the really nice recent books is *Creating Confident Writers* by Troy Hicks and Andy Schoenborn. They have been involved in the Chippewa River Writing Project, a site of the influential National Writing Project at Central Michigan University, and their approach to student-centered writing instruction is really promising.

In my teaching life at the University of Michigan-Flint, I think I talked to every member of the English department at some time or other about writing and teaching writing. Not everyone agreed with everyone else (or with me) on every point, but it's the differences of opinion that make horse races—and writing programs. I especially value my conversations with our first two directors of writing, Lois Rosen and Robert Barnett, as well as colleagues Fred Svoboda, Stephanie Carpenter, Dave Larsen, Stephanie Roach, Jacob Blumner, Maureen Thum, Jan Furman, Stephen Bernstein, and Suzanne Knight. My students, too, taught me volumes that aren't in the teaching texts, particularly through their struggles, which often reminded me of my own. Writing isn't easy for most of us, and those difficulties, theirs and mine, inform much of what is in this book.

Many thanks to my editor at HarperCollins, Sara Nelson, for all her help with the book, and to my agent, Faith Hamlin, for always fighting in my corner. I would be lost without you.

Finally, something that didn't happen on a campus but couldn't have happened without one. Many years ago, a group of us, working writers and writing instructors, decided it might be fun to get together on Friday afternoons and exchange our work-in-progress with an eye toward making it better. Wine may or may not have been involved. There were poets and novelists and critical writers and a technical writer and some who didn't know exactly where we fit but were disposed to try various genres. There was pressure to produce but very little pressure to measure up to what others were doing. We weren't there to score points off each other, as sometimes happens in creative writing classes, but to lift one another up and find what worked best and what could be improved in each submission. The criticism could be sharp and shrewd but was never cruel. I learned more from the interactions with those dedicated and kind people than from all the teaching courses and pedagogical seminars I ever attended. It was a lively and devoted group for a number of years before other jobs and other duties pulled us in diverse directions, but I could not have written this book without the lessons I learned from Jack Helder, Etta Abrahams, Paul Somers, John Smolens, Mike Holaday, Ken Wiley, Michael Steinberg, Dick Thomas, and most especially Leonora Smith, with her generosity of spirit and her fabulous dining room table, perhaps the world's most elaborate editing desk. God be with the days!

Index

About the Author

Thomas C. Foster is the *New York Times* bestselling author of *How to Read Literature Like a Professor*, *Twenty-Five Books That Shaped America*, and *How to Read Poetry Like a Professor*. He is a retired professor of English at the University of Michigan-Flint, where he taught courses in modern literature, Greek and Roman literature, creative writing, and nonfiction writing. He has written several books on twentieth-century British and Irish fiction and poetry, and lives in East Lansing, Michigan.